Evelyn Sloppy

Frayed-Edge Fun

10 Cozy Quilts

Martingale™
& COMPANY

Frayed-Edge Fun: 10 Cozy Quilts
© 2002 by Evelyn Sloppy

Martingale & Company
20205 144th Avenue NE
Woodinville, WA 98072-8478
www.martingale-pub.com

Printed in China
07 06 05 04 03 02   8 7 6 5 4 3 2

Library of Congress Cataloging-in-Publication Data
Sloppy, Evelyn
    Frayed-edge fun: 10 cozy quilts / Evelyn Sloppy.
        p. cm.
    ISBN 1-56477-427-9
    1. Patchwork—Patterns. 2. Quilts. 3. Borders, Ornamental (Decorative arts) 4. Seams (Sewing) 5. Novelty fabrics. I. Title.
TT 835 .S554497 2002
746.46'041—dc21   2002003480

CREDITS

PRESIDENT	Nancy J. Martin
CEO	Daniel J. Martin
PUBLISHER	Jane Hamada
EDITORIAL DIRECTOR	Mary V. Green
MANAGING EDITOR	Tina Cook
TECHNICAL EDITOR	Laurie Baker
COPY EDITOR	Karen Koll
DESIGN DIRECTOR	Stan Green
ILLUSTRATOR	Robin Strobel
COVER AND TEXT DESIGNER	Trina Stahl
PHOTOGRAPHER	Brent Kane

MISSION STATEMENT

We are dedicated to providing quality products and service by working together to inspire creativity and to enrich the lives we touch.

Dedication

To my four grandchildren, Kylie, Brad, Cole, and Ireland, the one on the way, and any future ones, for whom I started making these snuggly, frayed-edge quilts. Their delight in receiving these quilts keeps me making them. The enthusiasm and joy for life that they feel is such an inspiration to me, and I love them all.

Acknowledgements

I wouldn't have tapped the creativity inside of me if it weren't for all the great quilting teachers and wonderful quilting books available to start me thinking "what if?" Even though I've never met many of the authors I admire, I feel as though I know them through their books. Thanks to all the authors who have written books that have inspired me and to all the teachers who have shared their special techniques with me, but an especially big thanks to Sharyn Craig for her innovative techniques and "what if?" ideas, Sally Schneider for all her scrap quilts and timesaving ideas, Judy Martin for her beautiful quilts and blocks, Donna Lynn Thomas for her color recipes, and Mary Tendall Etherington and Connie Tesene of Country Threads for their "Bull's Eye" quilt, which sparked my love for frayed-edge quilts.

Also, thanks go to Linda Taylor for teaching a machine quilting class that started me thinking about whole-cloth frayed appliqué. Thanks to all for sharing your creativity with me.

Contents

Introduction · 6

Quiltmaking Basics · 8

    Fabric · 8

    Batting · 8

    Supplies · 9

    Rotary Cutting · 10

    Making Templates · 10

Frayed-Edge Stitching

Techniques · 11

    Seams Inside Out · 11

    Frayed-Appliqué Piecing · 14

    Whole-Cloth Frayed Appliqué · 14

    Frayed Circles · 15

Quilt Finishing · 19

    Layering and Basting · 19

    Binding · 19

    Washing and Drying
        the Finished Quilt · 21

Projects

    Baby Rails · 22

    Bricks around the World · 25

    ABC ... 123 · 28

    Prairie Hearts · 35

    Vintage Nine Patch · 41

    Plaid Patches · 46

    Bears around the Corner · 50

    Baby Blues · 58

    Four-Patch Snuggler
        and Pillow · 63

    Forever Frayed · 71

About the Author · 79

Introduction

WHILE I WAS visiting a local quilt shop several years ago, I saw a quilt that beckoned me to come closer. I noticed, upon inspection, that the edges of the pieces were raw, unfinished. I had to reach out and touch it. I immediately loved the texture of the fabrics between my fingers and the old, worn look the frayed edges gave to the quilt. It was the "21st Century Bull's Eye" quilt from the book *Quilts from Aunt Amy* by Country Threads. Of course I had to have my own such quilt, and in short order, I did. It was so much fun to make. When I showed my finished "unfinished" quilt to my quilting group, my friends had to reach out and feel it, just as I had. Before long, we all had "Bull's Eye" quilts. Next I made one with squares instead of circles, and then, never liking to make the same quilt twice, started experimenting with even more settings.

Then I saw a quilt with the unfinished, clipped seams on the right side of the quilt. I knew this technique would fit in perfectly with my frayed-edge quilts, so I started experimenting with it. I found that if I made a narrower seam, the seams would fray and look like chenille when the quilts were washed and dried. Using this technique, I found that many of the quilts were completed when the piecing was finished; no quilting or binding was needed. This made the quilts even more appealing.

I started experimenting with different ways to introduce these raw edges to my quilts. In several, I didn't even do any piecing; I just sewed the cut pieces to a whole-cloth base for a really primitive look. With others, I sewed circles with frayed edges together to achieve a Cathedral Windows look. I had entered a new phase of quilting—not that I had abandoned my traditional quilting, but what a lovely addition this was.

My family started asking me to make them these worn, tattered quilts. They had such a warm, comfy feel to them; they were perfect for the lap quilts I loved to make and give away. These are the quilts that really get used. They are the ones my grandkids bring with them when they come to visit me. They know they don't have to take special care of these quilts. When they get dirty, we just wash and dry them, and they're ready to go again. I find them thrown all over the house—on the furniture, on the floor, occasionally with a dog sleeping on one. Quite often I find a child curled up with one, taking a breather from his or her busy day. Those are special moments. My grandkids and I have come to call these our "snuzzler" quilts. They always have one in tow when it's time for a bedtime story, and they usually fall asleep with one. I do believe they like these quilts the best. They all have special, more traditionally pieced quilts on their beds and walls that they treat with care. These more formal quilts take longer to make and may still be in use many years from now. But the snuzzler quilts are the ones they really use. I don't expect these to last for years, but that's OK, because I love making more. They are laundered often, with no special care, and seem to get even softer and cozier with use. They are the ones my husband and I use in the evening while reading by the fireplace. They make great gifts—for a friend recuperating from an illness, for a new baby, or just because.

Although I still love to make traditional quilts with lots of intricate piecing, I like to throw in these frayed quilts now and then for a change of pace. They are quick, easy, and fun to make. I find that when I need a break from a very tediously pieced quilt, making one of these frayed-edge quilts renews my spirit and makes me laugh and feel the joy of quilting again. So take a break and try making one of these snuggly quilts for a special person in your life. You probably won't stop at one.

DETAIL FROM: Forever Frayed (page 71)

Quiltmaking Basics

Fabric

SELECT HIGH-QUALITY, 100 percent–cotton fabrics. They hold their shape well and are easy to handle. For the techniques used in this book, use cottons that fray easily. Flannel is always a good choice, along with homespuns. However, don't feel you can't use other 100 percent–cotton fabrics. If you're in doubt about how much fabrics will fray, try out the intended frayed-edge technique on a sample before you cut out pieces for the entire quilt. Also, don't overlook used denim jeans that are 100 percent cotton. Pieces cut from discarded jeans fray beautifully, and it's a great way to recycle. They also look great when paired with plaid flannels. When making a quilt for a baby, be cautious of using fabrics that leave long threads as the baby might get his or her fingers tangled in the strands.

Yardage requirements are based on 42" of usable fabric after preshrinking. Make it a habit to preshrink your fabrics after you purchase them so they will be ready to sew when you are. To preshrink your fabrics, place all of the fabrics into the washing machine and fill the tub with water. Do not use any detergent. Let the fabrics soak for ten minutes and then run them through the spin cycle to remove the water. This method does not remove the sizing from the fabrics, so they do not ravel and tangle up with each other. Dry the fabrics in the dryer, then fold them neatly and store them. I do not press my fabrics until I am ready to use them.

Batting

FOR MANY of these projects, the batting is attached to the top and backing during the piecing process, so you need to select batting when you select fabrics. You have various batting choices.

When I am piecing the batting with the top and backing, I prefer a low-loft cotton batting, because cotton doesn't shift as much as a polyester batting. In some of the projects, the batting will show in the unfinished seam allowance, so color is also a consideration. If you are using pastel fabrics in your top, natural-color battings blend in well. If you are using medium- to dark-color fabrics, use a gray batting, or dye the batting a color that will blend with your fabrics. If you choose to dye the batting, use cotton batting and follow the dye manufacturer's instructions; polyester battings do not accept dye well. For projects where the batting is cut into pieces, it is perfectly acceptable to use batting scraps left over from another project, and it's a great way to use up odd pieces.

Another choice for batting is 100 percent–cotton flannel. Using flannel as the batting makes a denser, heavier quilt, and it is a great alternative for the techniques where the batting will be seen in the seam allowances. Because only the edges of the flannel will show, don't use your favorite, expensive pieces of flannel for batting. As long as the flannel blends with the top fabrics, it doesn't matter if it is a solid or a print. Maybe you have some pieces you don't really care for anymore. Use them here. You can also use leftover flannel scraps from other quilts. They don't all have to be from the same fabric. Not only will these flannels enhance your quilt, you'll feel good about finding a use for them.

Supplies

Needles. Use sewing-machine needles sized for cotton fabrics (size 70/10 or 80/12). You may also need hand-sewing needles (Sharps) for some finishing techniques, and if you choose to hand quilt you will need hand-quilting needles, called Betweens, in size 8, 9, or 10.

Pins. A good supply of glass- or plastic-headed pins is necessary. Long pins are especially helpful for pinning multiple layers together. If you plan to machine quilt, you will need to pin-baste the layers of the quilt together with rustproof, size 2 safety pins.

Pressing equipment. Iron your fabrics before you cut out the pieces. In the quilts in this book the seam allowances are finger-pressed open, with the exception of "ABC . . . 123," which is assembled in a more traditional manner and requires the use of an iron and pressing surface.

Rotary cutter, mat, and rulers. A rotary cutter with a 45 mm or 60 mm blade enables you to cut strips and pieces quickly. A self-healing cutting mat is essential to protect both the blade and the table on which you are cutting. Choose a mat that is no smaller than 18" x 24" so you can cut long strips on the straight or bias grain. You might also consider purchasing a smaller mat to use when working with scraps. Use a clear acrylic ruler to measure and to guide the rotary cutter. A 6" x 24" rotary ruler with standard ¼" increments and guidelines for marking and cutting 45° and 60° angles is a good choice. Using a specialized ruler improves cutting accuracy, makes quiltmaking more fun, and frees you from the matching and stitching frustrations that can result from inaccurate cuts.

Scissors. Use good-quality shears, and use them only for cutting fabric. Thread snips or embroidery scissors are handy for clipping threads.

Seam ripper. This little tool will come in handy if you find it necessary to remove a seam.

Sewing machine. Machine piecing does not require an elaborate sewing machine. All you need is a straight-stitch machine in good working order. Set the machine for a balanced straight stitch and adjust the tension, if necessary, to produce smooth, even seams. A puckered seam causes the fabric to curve, distorting the size and the shape of the piece you are stitching and ultimately the quilt you are making. For many of the quilts in this book, you will be sewing through several thicknesses of fabric and batting. A walking foot is very helpful for keeping the fabric layers smooth and helping to avoid puckers.

Template plastic. Clear or frosted template plastic is available at most quilt shops.

Temporary spray adhesive. This spray eliminates the need for pinning by temporarily bonding fabric to fabric or fabric to batting. Any residue will wash out when you wash the quilt.

Thread. For piecing, use a good-quality cotton or cotton-covered polyester thread. For hand appliqué, I like to use #8 pearl cotton or two strands of embroidery floss.

Water-soluble marker or chalk pencil. There are various fabric markers and pencils available. Follow the manufacturer's instructions for removing the marks, and always test the product on a piece of scrap fabric to make sure it will wash out.

Rotary Cutting

NOT ALL of the pieces for the quilts in this book can be rotary cut, but whenever possible, rotary cutting instructions are given. For those unfamiliar with rotary cutting, a brief introduction is provided below. For more detailed information, refer to *Shortcuts: A Concise Guide to Rotary Cutting* by Donna Lynn Thomas (Martingale & Company, 1999).

1. Fold the fabric in half lengthwise, matching the selvages. Align the grain lines as much as possible so that the crosswise grain line runs parallel to the cut edge and the lengthwise grain line runs parallel to the folded edge. Place the folded fabric on the cutting mat with the folded edge closest to you. Align a square ruler, such as a Bias Square®, along the folded edge of the fabric. Butt up a long, straight ruler to the left edge of the square ruler, just covering the uneven raw edges along the left side of the fabric, as shown.

   Remove the square ruler and cut along the right edge of the long ruler. Discard the cut strip. (Reverse this entire procedure if you are left-handed.)

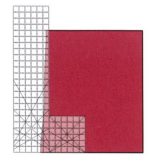

2. Measuring from the straightened edge, cut strips the required width. For example, to cut a 3"-wide strip, align the 3" ruler marking with the edge of the fabric.

3. Turn each strip horizontally and trim the selvage ends. Cut each strip into pieces the desired size.

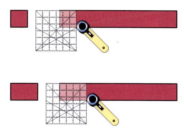

Making Templates

YOU WILL need to make templates for several of the quilts in this book. For some quilts, such as "ABC . . . 123" on page 28, the templates will be used to make appliqués that will be raw-edge stitched to the quilt top. For other quilts, such as "Baby Blues" on page 58, the templates will be used to make the pieces that will be stitched together to make the quilt. Patterns for creating the templates are given with each project. Seam allowances have already been added to the patterns where necessary.

To make the templates, place a piece of template plastic over the pattern and trace around the perimeter of the shape with a permanent marker. Label the template with the project name. Cut out the template on the outer line. Refer to the project for any other specific instructions for marking and cutting out the templates.

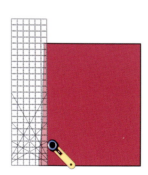

Frayed-Edge Stitching Techniques

Y OU WILL USE the four techniques given here to make the projects throughout the book. They are not traditional piecing techniques, so pay close attention to the seam-allowance width and to whether the pieces are assembled with the top fabrics or the backing fabrics right sides together. Be sure to follow the instructions given with each technique to make a sample before cutting out the pieces for the entire quilt. Making a sample is a good way to audition the fabrics and to make sure they will fray the desired amount.

Seams Inside Out

FOR THIS technique, the quilt top, batting, and backing pieces are first assembled into "sandwiches." Then the sandwiches are stitched together, backing fabric to backing fabric, so that the seam allowances appear on the top side of the quilt; the back of the quilt will have finished seams. When the piecing is done, the exposed seam allowances are clipped and the quilt is washed and dried, causing the raw edges to fray and create a chenille look. There is no need to bind the quilt unless you want to, because the outer edges are also clipped.

Flannels always work well for this technique, but don't overlook other options. A denim top and flannel backing make a great combination. I don't use a batting when I use denim because the denim is very heavy. "Baby Rails" was made with quilting cottons and a low-loft cotton batting. Also, consider using flannel in place of a traditional batting. I used a flannel batting in "Bricks around the World."

Chain piecing, which saves time and thread, is not appropriate for most frayed-edge techniques, but it does work well with the seams-inside-out technique. To chain piece, stitch the first pair of pieces from cut edge to cut edge using twelve to fifteen stitches per inch. At the end of the seam, stop sewing but don't cut the thread. Feed the next pair of pieces under the presser foot, as close as possible to the first pair. (A walking foot is very helpful for the seams-inside-out technique.)

Continue feeding pieces through the machine without cutting the threads between pairs. When all the pieces are sewn, remove the chain from the machine and clip the threads between the pairs.

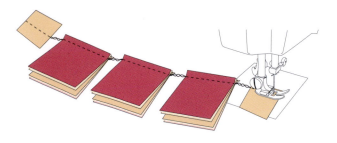

To make a seams-inside-out sample:

1. Cut 4 squares each from the top fabric, bottom fabric, and batting, each 4" x 4".

2. Layer the squares in the following order: bottom square, wrong side up; batting (it doesn't matter which side is up, even if you use flannel); top square, right side up. This is your "sandwich." Using straight pins, pin the layers together in the center of the square. Make 4.

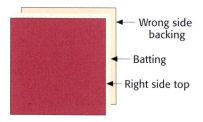

— Wrong side backing

— Batting

— Right side top

3. Place 2 "sandwiches" together, backing fabric to backing fabric. Stitch 1 side together, using a ½" seam allowance. Repeat with the other 2 sandwiches.

½" seam allowance

Top

4. Finger-press the seam allowances open. They will lie on the top side of your pieced units.

5. Place the 2 pieced units together, backing fabric to backing fabric. Align the seams. Stitch along the edge that runs perpendicular to the first seam, using a ½" seam allowance. Finger-press the seam allowance open.

½" seam allowance

6. Stitch ½" from the edges of the four-patch block. Turn your piece over and you will see that the back has finished seams.

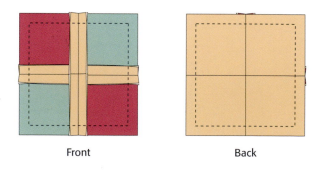

Front   Back

7. Now it's time to get out a sharp pair of scissors that are comfortable to work with and start clipping the seam allowances, including those around the block edges. Make clips about ¼" apart, clipping almost to the stitching line. This will make the raw edges fray once they are washed and dried. Take your time clipping, and clip for short periods of time so that it doesn't become a tedious chore. I enjoy this part and work on it in the evenings while watching TV, talking on the phone, or riding in the car. It is very important to have a comfortable pair of scissors. Special scissors are made for arthritic hands, and I especially like the spring-loaded scissors because they have no thumbholes.

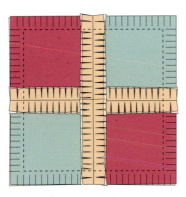

Clip seams ¼" apart,
almost to the stitching line.

8. At this point your sample still won't look like much. Don't worry. These seams-inside-out quilts don't take on their true character until they have been laundered. Run your sample through a wash cycle and dry it in the dryer. When you take it out, the unfinished seams will have frayed and tangled together in a beautiful chenille look.

Tip

Experiment with the width of the seam allowance for different looks. I like the chenille effect, so I take ½" wide (or less) seams. If you want a longer, fringed look, you'll need to adjust the cut size of the block pieces to reflect a ¾" or 1" seam allowance and then stitch the appropriate width seam. For example, the sample block squares that we originally cut 4" x 4" would finish to 3" x 3" if you used the ½" wide seam allowance called for in the instructions (4" minus twice the seam allowance equals 3"). If you want the seam allowance to be 1" wide, take the finished square size and add twice the desired seam allowance (3" + 2" = 5"). Cut your squares 5" x 5" and take a 1" seam.

Frayed-Appliqué Piecing

THIS IS the technique used in the "21st Century Bull's Eye" quilt that got me started on frayed-edge patchwork. The technique involves simply placing a cut piece of fabric, or appliqué, on top of a piece of the background fabric, both right sides up, and stitching ¼" from the raw edges of the cut piece. The background pieces are then stitched together. The unfinished edges of the cut pieces will fray when the quilt is washed and dried. For "ABC . . . 123" on page 28 I assembled the blocks in a traditional manner to complete the quilt top and then layered the top with backing and batting and quilted it. For "Prairie Hearts" on page 35, I stitched the cut pieces, background fabric, batting, and backing together in one step and then stitched the blocks together using the seams-inside-out technique. No additional quilting was needed.

Most 100 percent–cotton fabrics work well for frayed-appliqué piecing. Some fabrics, such as homespuns, will fray almost back to the stitching, while others will fray just a small amount. Decide which look you like best for the quilt you are making by stitching a sample.

To make a frayed-appliqué-piecing sample:

1. Cut a 6" x 6" square from the base fabric; then cut a smaller circle from the fabric that will be placed on top of the base.

2. Using straight pins, pin the circle on top of the base fabric with both fabrics right side up. Stitch ¼" from the circle edge.

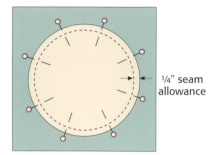

¼" seam allowance

3. Wash the sample in your washing machine and dry it in your dryer. It will come out of the dryer with lots of tangled, loose threads. Don't panic. This is part of the fraying process. Take your scissors and give your quilt a haircut. You can trim as little or as much as you like. Over the next several washings you may have to trim more loose threads, although it won't be nearly as much as the first time.

Whole-Cloth Frayed Appliqué

THIS TECHNIQUE is much the same as frayed-appliqué piecing, but the cut pieces are applied to a whole-cloth base—one large piece of background fabric with no seams—that has been layered with batting and backing. You do the quilting as you stitch down the cut pieces.

The base fabric will appear much the same as the background fabric in a pieced block. In "Bears around the Corner" (page 50) I used muslin for the base. "Plaid Patches" (page 46) has a print fabric for the base. Whether you use a print or a solid is up to you, but if your finished quilt measures wider than 40", you'll need to start with a 90" or 108" wide fabric for the base.

Use a water-soluble marker or chalk pencil to mark the base fabric with a grid pattern. The pattern provides guidelines for placing your cut pieces. Once the base fabric is marked, refer to "Layering and Basting" on page 19 to layer the whole-cloth top with batting and backing.

Now you are ready to apply the cut pieces. A temporary spray adhesive works well for this, or you can just pin the pieces to the top. I work with a few pieces at a time, sew them on, and then do a few more. If the cut pieces are stitched to the base in rows, as with "Plaid Patches" on page 46, start at the top of the quilt and work your way down. "Bears around the Corner" is a medallion-style quilt, so it is best to begin in the center and work your way out. Use a walking foot when sewing on the pieces to avoid puckers and help keep the layers smooth. Stitch your cut pieces onto the base, ¼" from the outer edges. If you are machine stitching, you may have to move the quilt as you stitch around each piece. To avoid turning the quilt frequently, try free-motion quilting. If you enjoy hand quilting, try using #8 pearl cotton and a long running stitch to attach the pieces to the top. This will go much faster than traditional hand quilting, and it really adds to the primitive look of your quilt.

When you have finished sewing all the cut pieces onto the basted quilt, attach the binding. Remove the grid marks, following the manufacturer's instructions. Launder the quilt. Trim the loose, tangled threads after washing and drying, and your quilt is done.

If you don't like working with the bulk of the basted layers, you can take a more traditional approach to assembling the quilt by stitching the cut pieces onto the marked whole-cloth base and then layering the quilt top with batting and backing. Tie or quilt the layers together to secure them.

To make a sample, follow the instructions for "Frayed-Appliqué Piecing" on page 14.

Tip

If you have access to a short-arm or long-arm quilting machine or one of the new Handi Quilters, whole-cloth frayed appliqué is especially quick and easy.

Frayed Circles

THIS TECHNIQUE is based on the Orange Peel and Robbing Peter to Pay Paul patterns that date back to the early 1800s. The pattern looks complicated with all of its interlocking circles, but it is actually quite easy using the frayed-circles technique.

No batting is used with this technique, so I find that flannel works best for the top and backing because the two layers create a very dense, heavy quilt. For a lighter-weight quilt, use quilting cottons, but remember that the frayed edges won't be as thick as when using flannel. The backing fabric will fold over to the front to form the arcs and will be seen as part of the quilt top, so choose contrasting fabrics that look good together. This technique looks lovely when done in just two fabrics, or you can make it completely scrappy. Only the backing fabric will be seen on the back. No additional quilting is needed, and no binding is required.

To make a frayed-circle sample:

1. Cut one 8" x 16" rectangle each from the top and backing fabrics. Place the rectangles wrong sides together, aligning the outer edges.

2. Trace the circle and square patterns on pages 61 and 62 onto template plastic. The circle cutting and stitching patterns are nested inside of each other, so be sure to make 2 separate templates. Mark the outer edges of the stitching-circle pattern on the cutting-circle template. Cut out the templates on the outer lines.

3. Using the stitching template and a water-soluble marker or chalk pencil, trace 2 circles on the top fabric rectangle, leaving at least 1" of space around each circle.

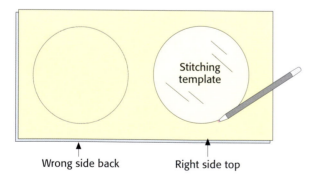

Wrong side back   Right side top

4. Place the square template over each of the marked circles so that the corners align with the circle edges. Trace around the square.

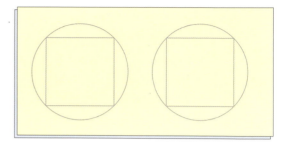

5. Using straight pins, pin the top and backing fabrics together to keep them from shifting. Sew completely around each circle on the drawn line. The stitching will show on the top and backing fabrics so be sure to use a thread color that matches both fabrics. Place the cutting template over each circle, aligning the stitching-template line with the stitching. Trace around each circle. Cut out the circles on the cutting-template line.

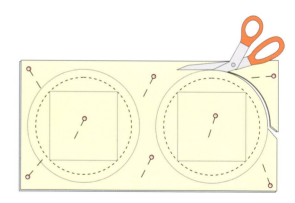

6. Place 2 circle units together, backing fabric to backing fabric. Place a pin through the top right corner of the drawn square and align it with the corresponding corner on the bottom circle. Repeat with the bottom right corner. When the points are aligned, pin the circles

together along the vertical line. Remove the alignment pins at the corners. Stitch along the vertical line, backstitching at the beginning and end of the stitching line. Do not stitch through the seam allowances.

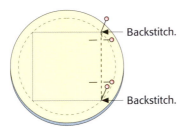

Backstitch.

Backstitch.

7.   Open out the sewn circles so the top fabric is right side up. Fold the 2 flaps created by the seam down onto the circles. Stitch the flaps down, stitching over the previous stitching line.

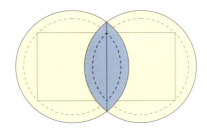

8.   Clip the seam allowances along the stitched-down flaps and the circle outer edges. Make clips about ¼" apart, clipping almost to the stitching line.

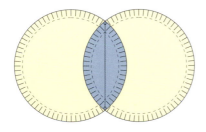

9.   Wash and dry the stitched piece.

Tip

You can make the circles for a frayed-circles quilt in any size. To make the square that corresponds with your circle size, divide the circle diameter by 1.4. This will be the size square you need. Once you have cut out your square template, place it inside your circle template. The edges of the square should fall right on the edges of the circle. If it extends beyond the circle, trim it a little, making sure to keep it square.

To stitch the circles (or ovals) into rows and stitch the rows together:

1.   Refer to the instructions for the desired project to make the templates and cut the required pieces from the top and backing fabrics.

2.   Stitch 2 pieces together as described above for the sample. Continue adding pieces to the right-hand side of the row until you have the required number of pieces in the row. Add each new piece to the previous piece, and then sew the flaps down. Make as many separate rows as you need for the project.

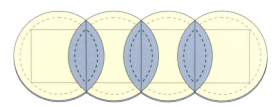

Stitch together all the circles in the row; then sew down the flaps.

3. To join the rows, place 2 rows together, backing fabric to backing fabric. Beginning at one end, place a pin through the top right corner of the square (or diamond) that was drawn inside the circle and align it with the corresponding corner on the bottom circle. Repeat with the top left corner of the same circle. When the points are aligned, pin the pieces together along the horizontal line. Remove the alignment pins at the corners. Holding the seam allowances of the vertical arcs out of the way, stitch along the horizontal line, backstitching at the beginning and end of the stitching line. Do not stitch through the seam allowances, and do not stitch down the flaps at this time. Stitch the next circle in each row together in the same manner. Continue stitching the circles together in order horizontally until the rows are stitched together.

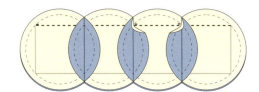

Fold vertical flaps out of the way and stitch each circle.

4. Open out the rows and fold the horizontal flaps down. Beginning at the edge, stitch alternating flaps down in one continuous line as shown, following the previous stitching line. Be sure to hold the vertical flaps out of the way as you stitch. End stitching at the opposite edge. Stitch the loose flaps down in the same manner.

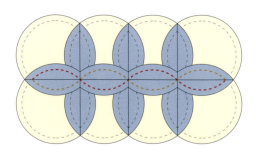

- - - First line of stitching
- - - Second line of stitching

Tip

You may find it easier to sew the rows together if you clip the seam allowances on the vertical flaps first.

5. Continue adding rows, always adding the rows so the bulk of the quilt is to the left of the machine. After adding the last row, you may leave the outer circle flaps unfolded to create a scalloped edge, or you may fold them down and topstitch them for a straight edge. The choice is yours.

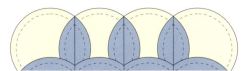

Outer edges left scalloped

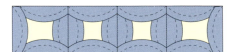

Outer edges folded down and topstitched

6. Now it's time to clip. With a comfortable pair of sharp scissors, clip all the unfinished seam allowances. Make clips about ¼" apart, clipping almost to the stitching line.

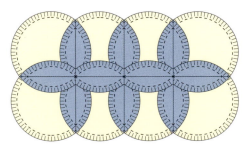

Clip all seams almost to stitching line.

7. Wash and dry the quilt. The raw edges will not fray together until this is done, so make sure you do this as soon as you have finished clipping. No batting, no binding. You're done!

Quilt Finishing

Y OU WILL BE finished with most of these quilts after you stitch the rows together, but for "ABC . . . 123" (page 28) and the whole-cloth–frayed-appliqué quilts (pages 46–57) you will need to know how to layer the quilt top with the batting and backing. No additional quilting is needed for these quilts either, with the exception, again, of "ABC . . . 123." For that quilt, or if you'd like to add additional quilting to any of the other quilts, I suggest you consult a basic machine-quilting book, such as *Machine Quilting Made Easy* by Maurine Noble (That Patchwork Place, 1994). Two techniques for binding the quilt edges are given in this section (pages 19–21).

Layering and Basting

1. Cut the quilt backing and batting to the sizes indicated in the project cutting instructions. If needed, stitch the backing pieces together to make one large piece that is at least 2" larger than the quilt top on all sides.

2. Lay the backing, wrong side up, on a flat, clean surface. Secure it with masking tape in several places along the edges to keep it smooth and taut. Be careful not to stretch the backing out of shape.

3. Spread the batting over the backing, smoothing out any wrinkles.

4. Center the finished or marked quilt top over the batting. Smooth out any wrinkles and make sure the quilt-top edges are parallel to the edges of the backing.

5. Pin-baste the layers together, using safety pins placed approximately 6" to 8" apart.

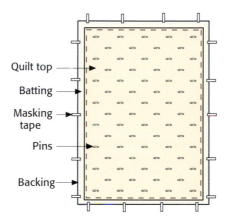

Quilt top →
Batting →
Masking tape →
Pins →
Backing →

Binding

FRENCH BINDING

1. Cut binding strips as indicated in the project instructions. For straight-cut French binding, cut the binding strips 2½" x 42" across the width of the folded fabric.

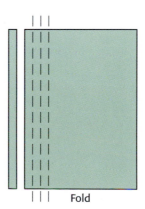

Fold

For bias-cut French binding, open up the fabric and lay it flat. Align the 45° line on your rotary cutting ruler with one of the selvage edges of the fabric. Cut along the ruler edge and trim off the corner. Cut 2½" wide strips, measuring from the edge of the initial bias cut.

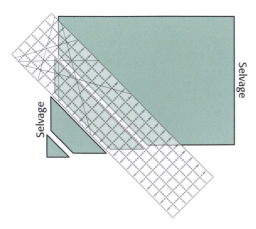

2. Stitch the binding strips together to make one long strip. Join strips at right angles, right sides together, and stitch across the corner as shown. Trim excess fabric and press the seams open.

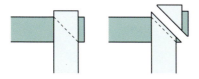

3. Cut one end of the strip at a 45° angle. Press under the angled end ¼". Press the strip in half lengthwise, wrong sides together.

4. Trim the batting and backing ¼" from the edges of the quilt top.

5. Starting on one side of the quilt and using a ¼" wide seam allowance, stitch the binding to the quilt, keeping the raw edges even with the quilt top edge. End the stitching ¼" from the corner of the quilt and backstitch. Clip the thread.

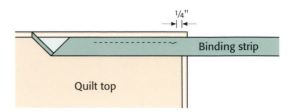

6. Turn the quilt so you will be stitching down the next side. Fold the binding up, away from the quilt, with raw edges aligned. Fold the binding back down onto itself, even with the edge of the quilt top. Beginning at the edge, stitch the binding to the quilt, stopping ¼" from the next corner. Backstitch and remove the quilt from the machine. Repeat the process on the remaining edges and corners of the quilt.

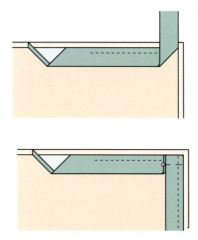

7. When you reach the beginning of the binding, stop stitching. Overlap the starting edge of the binding by about 1" and cut away any excess binding, trimming the end at a 45° angle. Tuck the end of the binding into the fold and finish the seam.

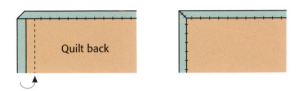

8. Fold the binding over the raw edges of the quilt to the back of the quilt, with the folded edge covering the row of machine stitching. Blindstitch the binding in place. A miter will form at each corner. Blindstitch the mitered corners in place.

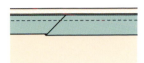

FRAYED-EDGE BINDING

1. Cut binding strips as indicated in the project cutting instructions. Follow step 2 of "French Binding," above, to stitch the strips into one long strip if necessary.

2. Measure the quilt-top top edge and cut a strip approximately 2" longer than this measurement. Press the strip in half lengthwise, wrong sides together.

3. Enclose the top edge of the quilt in the pressed binding strip. Pin the binding in place. Stitch ¼" from the binding raw edges. Trim the ends even with the quilt sides.

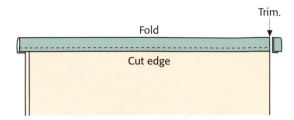

4. Repeat with the remaining 3 sides.

Washing and Drying the Finished Quilt

THESE QUILTS are not complete until they have gone through a cycle in the washer and dryer to fluff up and fray the raw edges. Just run the quilt through a complete wash cycle, using detergent in the water, then dry it in the dryer. Depending on the technique you used, you may need to trim any long strings from the raw edges.

Baby Rails

FINISHED QUILT SIZE: 46" x 46" · FINISHED BLOCK SIZE: 9" x 9" · TECHNIQUE: Seams inside out

This quilt goes together so quickly and feels so scrumptious you probably won't stop at one.
I used pastel-colored quilting cottons and natural-colored batting, but you'd never believe it wasn't
flannel just by looking at it. I also used two different color combinations of three fabrics each for the
blocks and one fabric for the sashing strips, but you can easily make this as scrappy as you want.
Just cut 150 total rectangles from fabric scraps and piece them together randomly.
Notice that all the seams are offset to avoid extra bulk and for ease in sewing the seams.

Materials

(42" wide fabric)

If you are using scraps, refer to "Cutting" for the number of pieces needed and the size of each piece.

- ¾ yd. each of 3 pink prints and 3 blue prints for blocks
- 1⅛ yds. of coordinating print for sashing
- 46" x 72" piece of batting

Cutting

All measurements include ½" wide seam allowances.

From *each* of the pink and blue prints, cut:
- 5 strips, 4" x 42". Crosscut each strip into 4 rectangles, 4" x 10" (120 total). You will use 116 rectangles and have 4 left over.

From the coordinating print, cut:
- 9 strips, 4" x 42". Crosscut the strips into 34 rectangles, 4" x 10".

From the batting, cut:
- 75 rectangles, 4" x 10"

Instructions

Refer to "Seams Inside Out" on page 11.

1. Using the pink-print rectangles, blue-print rectangles, coordinating-print rectangles, and batting rectangles, layer 75 "sandwiches," placing the same print on the top and bottom of the sandwich. Pin each sandwich through the center to secure the layers.

2. Using a ½" seam allowance, stitch 2 blue-print sandwiches and 1 pink-print sandwich together as shown. Finger-press the seam allowances open. Make 8 more blocks with the same print combination (color combination I). In the same manner, stitch together 1 sandwich each of the remaining 2 pink-print and 1 blue-print sandwiches. Make 9 blocks in this color combination (color combination II). You will use the remaining pink- and blue-print sandwiches, as well as the coordinating-print sandwiches, as sashing.

3. To make rows 1, 3, and 5, stitch together 2 color-combination-I blocks, 2 color-combination-II blocks, and 3 coordinating-print sashing strips as shown. You may orient the colors in each block in any manner desired. Press the seam allowances open.

Rows 1, 3, and 5

4. To make row 2, stitch together 2 color-combination-I blocks, 1 color-combination-II block, and 4 coordinating-print sashing strips as shown. Orient the colors in each block as desired. Stitch one of the remaining pink- or blue-print sandwiches to each end.

Row 2

5. To make row 4, stitch together 1 color-combination-I block, 2 color-combination-II blocks, and 4 coordinating-print sashing strips as shown. Orient the colors in each block as desired. Stitch one of the remaining pink- or blue-print sandwiches to each end.

Row 4

6. Stitch the rows together as shown.

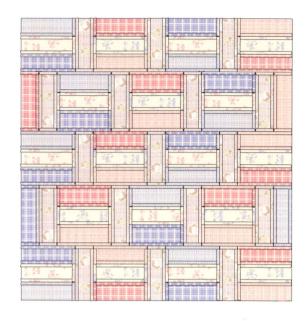

7. Stitch ½" from the quilt outer edges. Clip all of the seam allowances, as well as the outside edges of the quilt. Make clips about ¼" apart, clipping almost to the stitching line.

8. Refer to "Washing and Drying the Finished Quilt" on page 21 to wash and dry the quilt. There is no quilting or binding to do, so the quilt is finished!

Bricks around the World

FINISHED QUILT SIZE: 52" x 55" · FINISHED BLOCK SIZE: 3" x 6" · FINISHED HALF-BLOCK SIZE: 3" x 3"

TECHNIQUE: Seams inside out

*What a fun, scrappy quilt to make! By making the sandwiches so the top and backing fabrics
are the same, you create a truly reversible quilt. I used light and dark flannels instead of regular batting
for this quilt. Use up scraps, or maybe some pieces you wonder why you ever bought. Only the edges will
show, so even the color isn't that important. I used a dark brown piece with my dark bricks and a solid
cream flannel with my light bricks. If you want to use regular batting, the light color will not blend in
with the dark bricks; try dying half of it a dark color to use with the dark bricks.*

Materials

(42" wide fabric)

*If you are using scraps, refer to "Cutting" for the number of
pieces needed and the size of each piece.*

- ½ yd. *each* of 8 assorted dark flannel prints for
  bricks
- ½ yd. *each* of 8 assorted light flannel prints for
  bricks
- 2 yds. dark flannel for batting
- 2 yds. light flannel for batting

Cutting

All measurements include ½" wide seam allowances.

**From *each* of the 8 assorted dark flannel
prints, cut:**

- 2 strips, 7" x 42". Crosscut the strips to make a
  total of:
  - 144 rectangles (72 matching pairs),
    4" x 7", for bricks
  - 16 squares (8 matching pairs), 4" x 4", for
    half bricks

**From *each* of the 8 assorted light flannel
prints, cut:**

- 2 strips, 7" x 42". Crosscut the strips to make a
  total of:
  - 146 rectangles (73 matching pairs),
    4" x 7", for bricks
  - 16 squares (8 matching pairs), 4" x 4", for
    half bricks

From the dark flannel for batting, cut:

- 9 strips, 7" x 42". Crosscut the strips into:
  - 72 rectangles, 4" x 7", for dark-brick
    batting
  - 8 squares, 4" x 4", for dark–half brick
    batting

From the light flannel for batting, cut:

- 9 strips, 7" x 42". Crosscut the strips into:
  - 73 rectangles, 4" x 7", for light-brick
    batting
  - 8 squares, 4" x 4", for light–half brick
    batting

Instructions

Refer to "Seams Inside Out" on page 11.

1. Using the 4" x 7" dark bricks and dark batting rectangles, layer 72 "sandwiches," placing the same print on the top and bottom of the sandwich. Pin each sandwich in the center to secure the layers. Repeat with the 4" x 4" dark half bricks and dark batting squares. In the same manner, layer the light bricks and light batting rectangles and the light half bricks and light batting squares.

2. Stitch the brick and half brick sandwiches together end to end in the order shown to make the rows. Finger-press the seam allowances open.

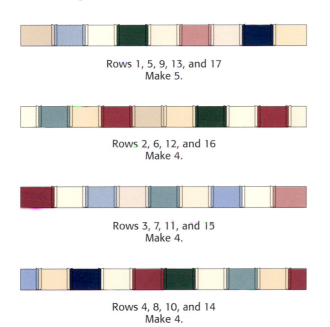

Rows 1, 5, 9, 13, and 17
Make 5.

Rows 2, 6, 12, and 16
Make 4.

Rows 3, 7, 11, and 15
Make 4.

Rows 4, 8, 10, and 14
Make 4.

3. Stitch the rows together.

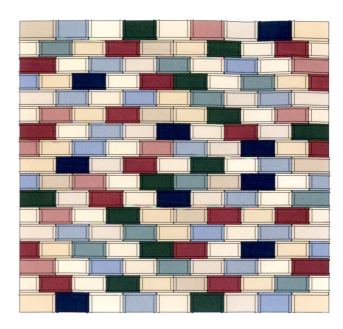

4. Stitch ½" from the quilt outer edges. Clip all of the seam allowances, as well as the outside edges of the quilt. Make clips about ¼" apart, clipping almost to the stitching line.

5. Refer to "Washing and Drying the Finished Quilt" on page 21 to wash and dry the quilt. There is no quilting or binding to do, so the quilt is finished!

ABC . . . 123

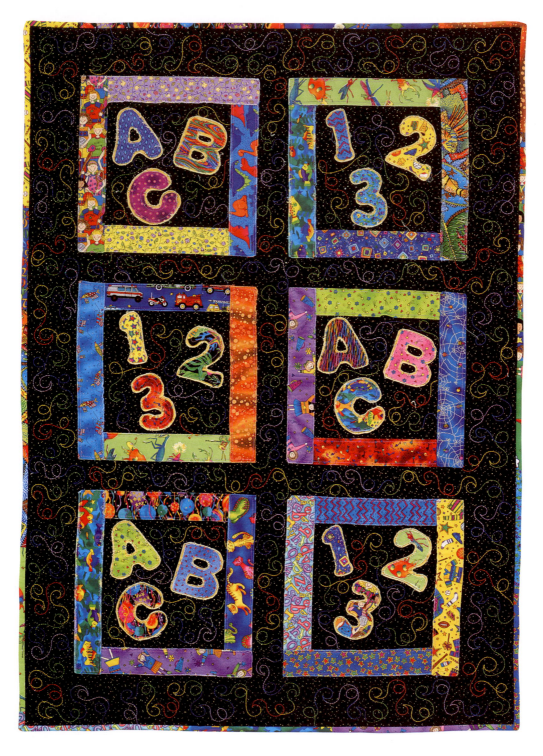

*Children will love the bright colors and the soft, worn edges of this fun quilt. Use the frayed-
appliqué-piecing technique to stitch the colorful pieces to a dark base fabric for truly spectacular results.
Be sure to cut the border strips along the lengthwise grain as instructed so that you do not
have to piece them and so that they are more stable and less likely to stretch out of shape.*

Materials

(42" wide fabric)

*If you are using scraps, refer to "Cutting" for the number of
pieces needed and the size of each piece.*

- ½ yd. bright yellow solid for appliqué backgrounds
- 1 fat quarter *each* of 8 to 10 assorted bright prints for block appliqués, block borders, and binding
- 2⅛ yds. black print or solid for block background, sashing, and borders
- 1¾ yds. fabric for backing
- Crib-size batting (45" x 60")
- Template plastic
- Water-soluble marker or chalk pencil
- Temporary spray adhesive (optional)

Cutting

All measurements include ¼" wide seam allowances.

From the 8 to 10 assorted bright prints, cut a *total* of:

- 8 strips, 2" x 10½", for block borders
- 8 strips, 2" x 11¾", for block borders
- 8 strips, 2" x 13", for block borders

From the black print or solid, cut:

- 4 strips, 6" x 76½", along the lengthwise grain. Crosscut the strips to make:
  - 4 rectangles, 6" x 10½", for horizontal sashing
  - 1 strip, 6" x 41½", for vertical sashing
  - 2 strips, 6" x 26", for top and bottom borders
  - 2 strips, 6" x 52½", for side borders
- 1 strip, 10½" x 76½", along the lengthwise grain. Crosscut the strip to make 6 squares, each 10½" x 10½", for block background.

Instructions

Refer to "Frayed-Appliqué Piecing" on page 14.

1. Refer to "Making Templates" on page 10 to trace the appliqué patterns on pages 33 and 34 onto template plastic. The small patterns are nested inside the large patterns, so be sure to make 2 separate templates for each letter and number. Cut out each template.

2. Using the large templates and a water-soluble marker or chalk pencil, trace 3 of each letter and number onto the right side of the bright yellow solid fabric. Cut out each appliqué along the marked lines.

3. Using the small templates and a water-soluble marker or chalk pencil, trace 3 of each letter and number onto the right sides of the bright prints. Cut out each appliqué along the marked lines.

4. With right sides up, center each print appliqué over a yellow appliqué of the same shape. Approximately ¼" of the yellow appliqué should extend beyond the print appliqué edges. Pin the paired appliqués together or follow the manufacturer's instructions to spray-baste them together.

5. Referring to the photo, randomly arrange the A, B, and C appliqués on 3 of the 10½" x 10½" background squares. Repeat with the 1, 2, and 3 appliqués and the remaining background squares. Pin the appliqués in place on the blocks or spray-baste them in place following the manufacturer's instructions. Stitch the appliqués in place ¼" from the print appliqué edges.

6. With right sides together, alternately stitch 3 appliqué blocks and 2 horizontal sashing rectangles together in 2 vertical rows as shown, using a ¼" seam allowance. Press the seam allowances toward the sashing.

7. Working on the right side of the pieced rows, pin or spray-baste a 2" x 10½" block-border strip right side up over each seam. Position each strip so that it covers the seam ½" and so

that the majority of the strip is on the sashing rectangle. Stitch the strips in place ¼" from the strip long edges.

8. Stitch the pieced rows to each side of the 6" x 41½" vertical sashing strip, using a ¼" seam allowance. Press the seams toward the sashing.

9. Referring to step 7, pin or spray-baste a 2" x 11¾" block-border strip to the vertical seams of the top and bottom blocks and a 2" x 13" block-border strip to the vertical seams of the center blocks. Stitch the strips in place ¼" from the strip edges.

10. Using a ¼" seam allowance, stitch the top and bottom border strips to the top and bottom edges of the quilt top. Press the seams toward the borders. Referring to step 7, pin or spray-baste the remaining 2" x 11¾" block-border strips over the top and bottom block-border seams. Stitch the strips in place ¼" from the strip edges.

11. Using a ¼" seam allowance, sew side-border strips to the sides of the quilt top. Press the seams toward the borders. Referring to step 7, pin or spray-baste the remaining 2" x 13" block-border strips to the sides of the blocks along the border seams. Stitch the strips in place ¼" from the strip edges.

12. Refer to "Layering and Basting" on page 19 to layer the quilt top with batting and backing; baste the layers together.

13. Quilt as desired.

14. Cut the leftover bright prints into 2½" wide strips of varying lengths. Referring to "Binding" on page 19, stitch the strips together to make 1 continuous strip approximately 190" long. Bind the quilt edges using the French binding method.

15. Refer to "Washing and Drying the Finished Quilt" on page 21 to wash and dry the quilt. Trim any loose, tangled threads.

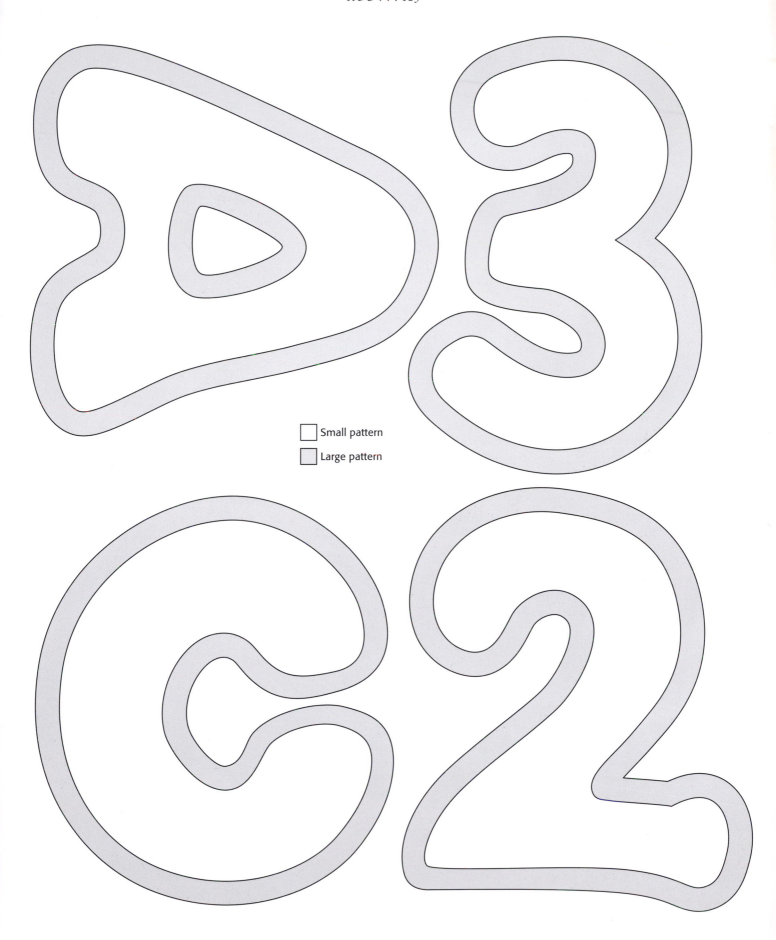

Small pattern

Large pattern

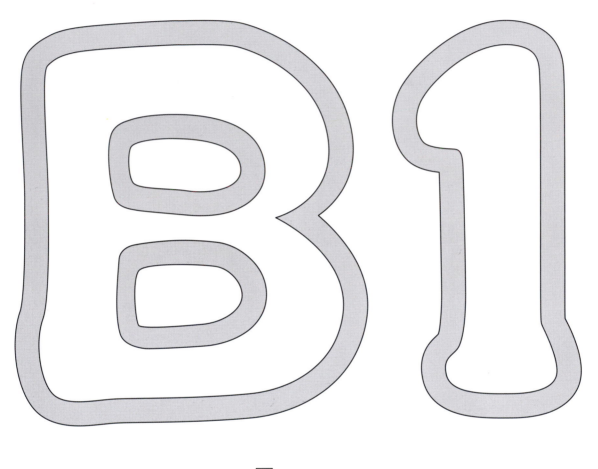

☐ Small pattern

▨ Large pattern

Prairie Hearts

FINISHED QUILT SIZE: 36" x 44" · FINISHED BLOCK SIZE: 18" x 18"

TECHNIQUES: Frayed-appliqué piecing, seams inside out

An assortment of red hearts on a yellow print background makes this quilt irresistible.
The wavy plaid strips cover up all the seam lines, so you can't tell where each block begins
and ends. Quilting as you piece makes this a quick-and-easy project.
Thanks to Maywood Studio for furnishing the fabrics.

Materials

(42" wide fabric)

IF YOU are using scraps, refer to "Cutting" for the number of pieces needed and the size of each piece.

- 1½ yds. fabric for backing
- 1½ yds. light-color print or solid for background
- 1¼ yds. red plaid for wavy strips and binding
- 1 fat quarter *each* of 4 assorted red prints
- Crib-size batting (45" x 60")
- Water-soluble marker or chalk pencil
- Temporary spray adhesive (optional)
- Tracing paper
- Template plastic

Cutting

All measurements include ½" wide seam allowances.

From the backing fabric, cut:
- 2 strips, 19" x 42". Crosscut the strips into 4 squares, 19" x 19", for blocks.
- 1 strip, 9" x 37", for upper unit

From the light-color print or solid, cut:
- 2 strips, 19" x 42". Crosscut the strips into 4 squares, 19" x 19", for background.
- 1 strip, 9" x 37", for upper unit

From the batting, cut:
- 4 squares, 18" x 18", for blocks
- 1 strip, 8" x 36", for upper unit

Instructions

Refer to "Seams Inside Out" on page 11 and "Frayed-Appliqué Piecing" on page 14.

1. Place a 19" x 19" backing square, wrong side up, on a flat surface. Center an 18" x 18" batting square on top of the backing, leaving ½" of backing on each side. Place a 19" x 19" background square, right side up, over the batting. Secure the layers with straight pins. Make 4.

——— Tip ———

*By making the batting smaller than
the backing and top, you will avoid
extra bulk in the seams when
the sandwiches are sewn together.*

2. From the plaid fabric, cut 11 strips with wavy edges, each approximately 1½" x 42". These are fun to cut freehand. They don't have to be exactly 1½" wide as long as the width doesn't vary too much. Cut 9 of the strips in half widthwise.

3. Using a water-soluble marker or chalk pencil, mark 3" from each side of each layered sandwich from step 1.

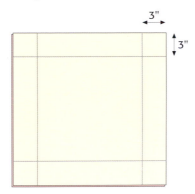

4. Center a halved wavy strip over the 2 horizontal lines on each block and then the 2 vertical lines. Pin the strips in place, or follow the manufacturer's instructions to spray-baste them in place. Stitch the strips in place ¼" from the strip long edges. Trim the strip ends even with the block edges.

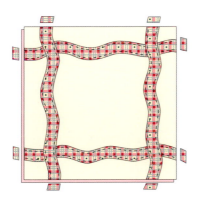

5. Fold the tracing paper in half. Trace the large and small heart patterns on page 40 onto the paper, aligning the paper fold line with the heart center lines. Cut out the hearts along the outer lines to make a complete pattern. With the hearts nested one inside the other as they are shown at right, lay the template plastic over the complete heart patterns. Referring to "Making Templates" on page 10, trace the hearts onto the template plastic. Cut out the hearts on the drawn lines.

6. Using a water-soluble marker or chalk pencil, trace a total of 4 large hearts and 9 small hearts onto the wrong side of the red prints. Cut out each heart on the drawn lines.

7. Place a large and small heart on each block, nesting a small heart inside each large heart as shown. Position the hearts on the blocks so that the bottom of the hearts will be pointing toward the center of the quilt when the blocks are assembled. Pin or spray-baste the hearts in place. Stitch the hearts in place ¼" from the heart outer and inner edges.

8. Stitch the blocks together into 2 horizontal rows of 2 blocks each, placing the backing fabrics together and using a ½" seam allowance. Finger-press the seam allowances open. Do not clip the seams.

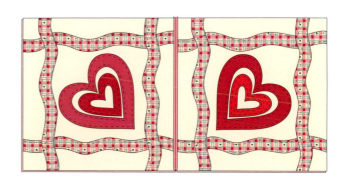

9. Center a halved wavy strip over the seam joining each pair of blocks. Pin or spray-baste the strips in place. Stitch the strips in place ¼" from the strip long edges. Trim the ends even with the block edges.

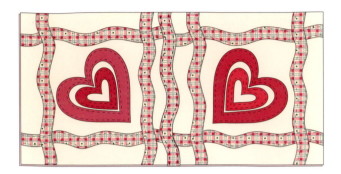

10. With backing fabric to backing fabric, stitch the rows together, using a ½" seam allowance. Finger-press the seam allowance open.

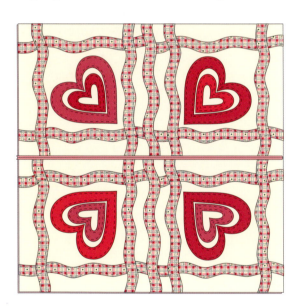

11. Center a full-length wavy strip over the seam joining the rows. Pin or spray-baste the strip in place. Stitch the strip in place ¼" from the strip long edges. Trim the ends even with the block edges.

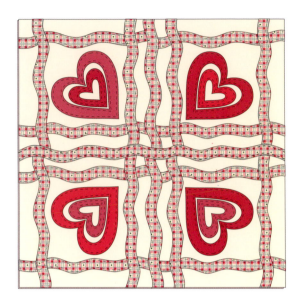

12. To make the top unit, refer to step 1 to layer the 9" x 37" backing rectangle, wrong side up, with the 8" x 36" batting rectangle and the 9" x 37" background rectangle, right side up. Secure the layers with straight pins.

13. Measure 18½" from either end to find the center of the sandwich; place a pin in the background fabric at the center point. Center one of the remaining 5 small hearts at the center point, placing the top of the heart 2" down from the top edge of the background rectangle. Place another heart on each end of the rectangle, 2½" from the end and 2" from the top edge. Center the remaining 2 hearts between the end and center hearts. Pin or spray-baste the hearts in place. Stitch the hearts in place ¼" from the inner and outer edges.

14. Stitch the top unit to the block unit, backing fabric to backing fabric, using a ½" seam allowance. Finger-press the seam allowance open.

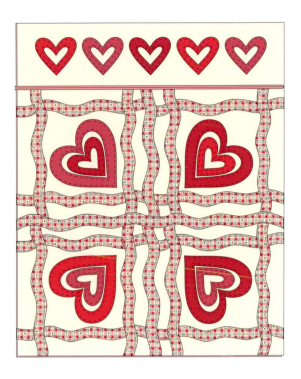

15. Center the remaining full-length wavy strip over the seam allowance. Pin or spray-baste the strip in place. Stitch the strip in place ¼" from the strip long edges. Trim the strip ends even with the quilt sides.

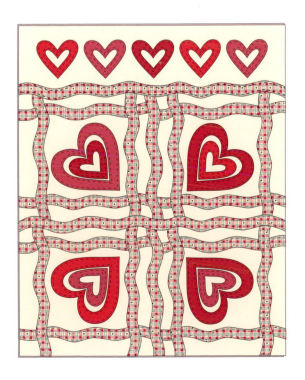

16. Trim the edges of the quilt top in a wavy pattern to match the strip edges. Referring to "Binding" on page 19, cut bias strips from the remaining red plaid fabric and join them together to make 1 continuous strip approximately 170" long. Stitch the binding to the quilt edges using the French binding method.

Tip

Any time your quilt has curved edges, you should cut the binding strips on the bias grain so the binding will stretch more easily. Straight-grain binding should be used only on straight edges.

17. Refer to "Washing and Drying the Finished Quilt" on page 21 to wash and dry the quilt. Trim any loose, tangled threads.

Large Heart
Cut 4.

Small Heart
Cut 9.

Place on fold.

Vintage Nine Patch

FINISHED QUILT SIZE: 55" x 66" · FINISHED BLOCK SIZE: 11" x 11"

TECHNIQUES: Frayed-appliqué piecing, seams inside out

Transform an old-fashioned favorite into a newfound friend when you use frayed-edge techniques to stitch up this warm and cuddly quilt. The classic Nine Patch block takes on new allure when strips are woven together and stitched to a square of base fabric using the frayed-appliqué-piecing technique. The base blocks are then sewn together using the seams-inside-out technique, so there are lots of fuzzy raw edges once the quilt is washed and dried.

Materials

(42" wide fabric)

If you are using scraps, refer to "Cutting" for the number of pieces needed and the size of each piece.

- 4 yds. tan for backing and binding
- 4½ yds. navy for block bases and sashing
- ⅜ yd. *each* of 8 assorted light blue and light brown plaids
- ⅜ yd. *each* of 8 assorted dark blue and dark brown plaids
- 60" x 72" rectangle of batting
- Temporary spray adhesive (optional)

Cutting

From the tan, cut:
- 10 strips, 13" x 42". Crosscut the strips into 30 squares, 13" x 13", for block backings.

From the navy, cut:
- 10 strips, 13" x 42". Crosscut the strips into 30 squares, 13" x 13", for block bases.
- 14 strips, 1¼" x 42", for sashing

From *each* of the 8 light blue and light brown plaids, cut:
- 1 strip, 9" x 42". Crosscut each strip into 12 rectangles (96 total), 3" x 9", for Woven Nine Patch blocks.

From *each* of the 8 dark blue and dark brown plaids, cut:
- 1 strip, 9" x 42". Crosscut each strip into 12 rectangles (96 total), 3" x 9", for Woven Nine Patch blocks.

From the batting, cut:
- 30 squares, each 11" x 11"

Instructions

Refer to "Seams Inside Out" on page 11 and "Frayed-Appliqué Piecing" on page 14.

1. Place a backing square, wrong side up, on a flat surface. Center a batting square over the backing. Place a 13" x 13" block base square over the batting, right side up. Align the backing and base square edges. Using straight pins, pin the layers together. Make 30 sandwiches.

2. Referring to "Woven Nine Patch Blocks" on page 45, make 30 Woven Nine Patch blocks. When assembling the blocks, place the light strips in the vertical positions and the dark strips in the horizontal positions, using light and dark strips from the same color family.

3. Center a Woven Nine Patch block right side up on the base fabric of each sandwich from step 1. There should be about 2" of base fabric showing around each Woven Nine Patch block. Place a pin in each corner of the Woven Nine Patch block to secure it to the sandwich.

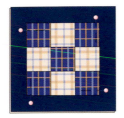

4. Using a walking foot, stitch a Woven Nine Patch block to each of the base sandwiches ¼" from the strip raw edges as shown, beginning at the dot and following the arrows around the block to stitch in a continuous line. You will stitch some areas twice.

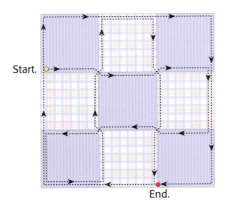

5. Lay the sandwiches out in 6 horizontal rows of 5 sandwiches each, alternating the block colors in each row. Referring to "Seams Inside Out" on page 11, stitch the blocks in each row together, backing fabric to backing fabric, using a 1" seam allowance. Finger-press the seam allowances open. Stitch the seam allowances in place ¼" from the seam allowance edges. Stitch the rows together, backing fabric to backing fabric, using a 1" seam allowance. Finger-press the seam allowances open. Stitch the seam allowances in place ¼" from the seam allowance edges. Do not clip the seam allowances.

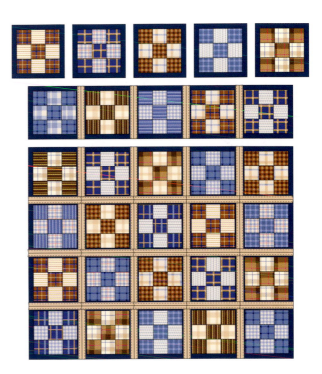

6. Stitch the 1¼" x 42" navy strips together end to end to make one long strip. From the strip, cut 5 strips, each 1¼" x 55", for the horizontal sashing, and 6 strips, each 1¼" x 66", for the vertical sashing. Center a horizontal sashing strip over each of the horizontal seams, leaving about 1" of seam allowance exposed at the end of each row. Pin the strips in place, or follow the manufacturer's instructions to spray-baste the strips in place. Stitch the strips in place

¼" from the long edges. Repeat to stitch the 1¼" x 66" sashing strips to the vertical seams.

7. To bind the quilt, trim about ½" of backing and base from the quilt-top outer edges to even them up. Fold the quilt outer edges to the top so they are even with the Woven Nine Patch blocks. Pin the folded edges in place; then stitch ¼" from the raw edges.

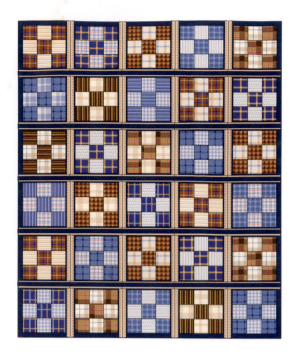

8. Refer to "Washing and Drying the Finished Quilt" on page 21 to wash and dry the quilt. Trim any loose, tangled threads.

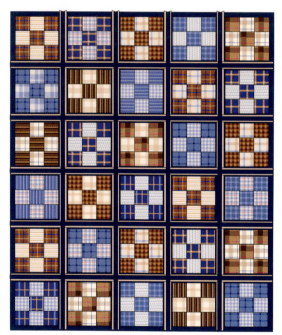

Woven Nine Patch Blocks

To make a Woven Nine Patch block:

1. Cut the number of light-color and dark-color strips the size indicated in the project instructions.

2. To make each block, select 3 identical light-color strips and 3 identical dark-color strips. With the right sides up, place the 3 light-color strips side by side on your pressing surface as shown.

3. Flip the middle strip down. Place 1 dark strip right side up horizontally across the 2 outer light-color strips, aligning the outside edges. Flip the middle strip back up into place.

4. Flip the 2 outer light-color strips up so the fold is aligned with the dark-color strip. Place another dark-color strip across the middle light-color strip. Flip the 2 outer light-color strips back down. Make sure the outer edges of all of the strips are aligned.

5. Flip the middle light-color strip up. Place the remaining dark-color strip across the 2 outer light-color strips. Flip the middle light-color strip back down into place.

6. Press the block. This will help the strips stay together.

Plaid Patches

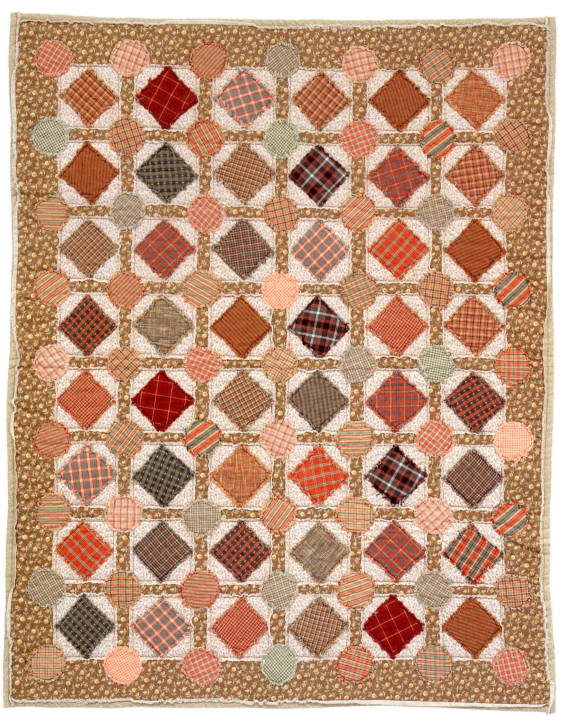

FINISHED QUILT SIZE: 35" x 45" • FINISHED BLOCK SIZE: 4¼" x 4¼"

FINISHED CIRCLE SIZE: 3" • TECHNIQUE: Whole-cloth frayed appliqué

*As soft and cuddly as a baby, this plaid-lover's quilt is a good design for learning
the whole-cloth—frayed-appliqué technique. Just stitch the squares and circles to the base fabric;
the base that shows through will look like the sashing and borders.
A clever frayed-edge binding quickly finishes this scrappy-looking quilt.*

Materials

(42" wide fabric)

- 1 yd. *total* of assorted medium- to dark-plaid scraps for block centers and circles
- 1⅝ yds. medium to dark print for whole-cloth base
- 1⅝ yds. fabric for backing
- ⅞ yd. light print for block bases
- ⅜ yd. fabric for frayed-edge binding*
- Crib-size batting (45" x 60")
- Template plastic
- Water-soluble marker or chalk pencil
- Temporary spray adhesive (optional)

*If you prefer a traditional French binding, you will need ½ yd. of fabric.

Cutting

From the medium- to dark-plaid scraps, cut:
- 48 squares, 3" x 3", for block centers

From the medium to dark print, cut:
- 1 rectangle, 40" x 50"

From the light print, cut:
- 6 strips, 4¼" x 42". Crosscut the strips into 48 squares, 4¼" x 4¼", for block bases.

From the binding fabric, cut:
- 5 strips, 1½" x 42"

Instructions

Refer to "Whole-Cloth Frayed Appliqué" on page 14.

1. Referring to "Making Templates" on page 10, trace the circle template pattern below onto template plastic and cut it out. Using the template and a water-soluble marker or chalk pencil, trace a total of 63 circles onto the wrong sides of the remaining medium- to dark-plaid scraps. Cut out the circles and set them aside.

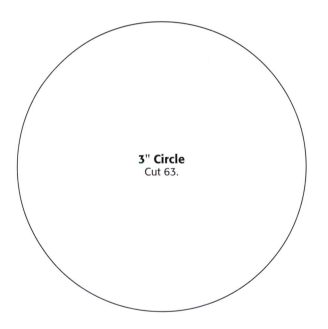

3" Circle
Cut 63.

2. Press the medium- to dark-print base fabric to remove any wrinkles. Using a water-soluble marker or chalk pencil, mark the grid on the fabric's right side as shown.

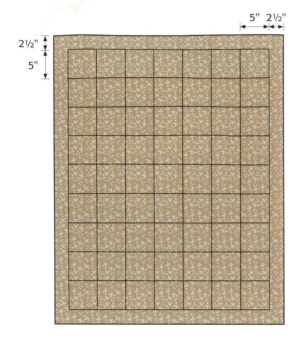

— *Tip* —

Use two rulers butted together to mark the long lines.

3. Refer to "Layering and Basting" on page 19 to layer the quilt top with batting and backing; baste the layers together.

4. Center 1 light-print square in each square of the left vertical row of the base grid, right sides up. Pin the squares in place, or follow the man-ufacturer's instructions to spray-baste them in place. Beginning at the upper edge of the first grid square and ending at the lower edge of the last grid square, stitch ¼" from each vertical side of the light-print squares. Do not stop between the squares. Continue adding vertical

rows in the same manner, working from the left side of the quilt to the right side of the quilt.

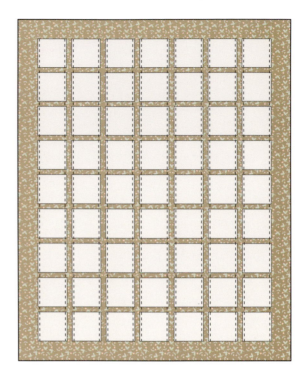

5. Stitch ¼" from the top and bottom edges of each square in the same manner.

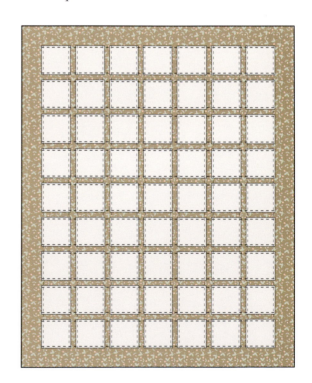

6. Pin or spray-baste a 3" x 3" medium- to dark-print square to each light-print square, setting the smaller squares right side up and on point inside the larger squares as shown. Stitch ¼" from the 3" square edges. You will have to turn the quilt to stitch all the way around the square, but this quilt is small so it shouldn't be too bulky. To avoid turning the quilt frequently, attach the darning foot, lower the feed dogs, and free-motion stitch the squares in place.

7. Beginning at the upper corner of the first horizontal row, center a circle, right side up, over each corner of each block. The circles will overlap more than one corner of adjacent squares. Pin or spray-baste the circles in place. Topstitch the circles in place ¼" from the circle edges.

Tip

If you are not comfortable machine stitching the pieces in place, hand stitch the squares and circles to the base using #8 pearl cotton and a long running stitch.

8. Trim the edges of the quilt top, batting, and backing 1" beyond the edges of the outer circles.

9. Referring to "Binding" on page 19, stitch the binding strips to the quilt edges using the frayed-edge binding technique.

10. Referring to "Washing and Drying the Finished Quilt" on page 21, wash and dry the quilt. Trim any loose, tangled threads.

Bears around the Corner

Finished quilt size: 67" x 67" · Finished block size: 9" x 9"

Technique: Whole-cloth frayed appliqué

*What a great quilt for a special guy! A cup of hot chocolate, a good book, and this quilt
really go together on a cold, winter evening. I was inspired to make this quilt after I took a long-arm
machine-quilting class from Linda Taylor. With Linda's teaching schedule and machine-quilting
business, she has little time to make her own quilts, so she makes them from start to finish on
a whole-cloth base on her quilting machine, much like you will do with this quilt.
I have also used a variation of her method for making the Woven Nine Patch blocks.*

Materials

(42" wide fabric)

- 2¼ yds. of 90" wide natural-colored muslin for quilt-top base
- 4½ yds. fabric for backing
- ⅜ yd. *each* of 8 light- to medium-plaid or print flannels
- ⅜ yd. *each* of 8 medium- to dark-plaid or print flannels
- ½ yd. brown flannel for bears and tree trunk
- 10" x 10" square of green flannel for treetop
- ⅞ yd. dark green flannel for bottom layer of inner and outer borders
- ¾ yd. light green flannel for top layer of inner and outer borders
- Twin-size batting (72" x 90")
- Water-soluble pen or chalk pencil
- Template plastic
- Temporary spray adhesive (optional)

Cutting

From the muslin, cut:

- 1 square, 72" x 72", for quilt-top base

From the backing, cut:

- 2 rectangles, 42" x 72"

From *each* of the 8 light- to medium-color flannels, cut:

- 1 strip, 9" x 42". Crosscut each strip into 12 rectangles (96 total), 3" x 9", for Woven Nine Patch blocks.

From *each* of the 8 medium- to dark-color flannels, cut:

- 1 strip, 9" x 42". Crosscut each strip into 12 rectangles (96 total), 3" x 9", for Woven Nine Patch blocks.

From the dark green flannel for inner and outer borders, cut:

- 12 strips, 2" x 42"

From the light green flannel for inner and outer borders, cut:

- 12 strips, 1½" x 42"

From the batting, cut:

- 1 square, 72" x 72"

Instructions

Refer to "Whole-Cloth Frayed Appliqué" on page 14.

1. Press the muslin base square to remove any wrinkles; then press the square in half vertically and horizontally to mark the center point. Using a water-soluble pen or chalk pencil, measure 20½" from the center point in all 4 directions as shown. Mark the point on the pressed lines. Connect the points to make the center square.

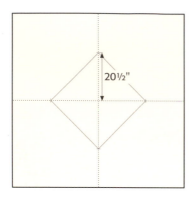

2. Mark a 2" border around the center square as shown. The outside edges of the border should measure 45" x 45".

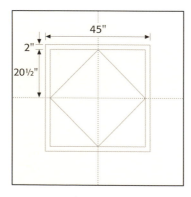

3. Referring to "Layering and Basting" on page 19, layer the marked quilt top with batting and backing; baste the layers together.

4. Referring to "Woven Nine Patch Blocks" on page 45, make 32 blocks: 20 dark blocks with the light strips in the vertical positions and the dark strips in the horizontal positions, and 12 light blocks with the dark strips in the vertical positions and the light strips in the horizontal positions.

Make 12 light blocks.   Make 12 dark blocks.

5. Gently pick up a dark Woven Nine Patch block and place it in one corner of the center square on the muslin base. Pin the block in several places to secure it. Using a walking foot, stitch the block in place ¼" from all of the block raw edges, stitching the 4 vertical lines first and then the 4 horizontal lines as shown.

Stitch 4 lines in one direction.   Stitch 4 new lines perpendicular to the first.

Tip

If you don't use a walking foot, you may get small puckers as you travel from one fabric to the next. However, when the quilt is laundered, it will shrink and the edges will fray, so the puckers won't be noticeable.

6. Referring to step 5, pin a dark Woven Nine Patch block in the remaining 3 corners of the center square and stitch them in place. Center and pin a dark block between each of the corner blocks, leaving approximately 1" between the block edges. Stitch the blocks in place.

7. Referring to "Making Templates" on page 10, trace the treetop, tree trunk, and bear template patterns on pages 56 and 57 onto template plastic and cut them out. Using the templates and a water-soluble marker or chalk pencil, trace 1 tree trunk and 4 bears (reverse 2) onto the wrong side of the brown flannel. Trace 1 treetop onto the wrong side of the green flannel. Cut out the appliqués on the drawn lines.

8. Position the treetop and tree trunk appliqués in the center opening of the base center square as shown. Pin the pieces in place, or follow the manufacturer's instructions to spray-baste them in place. Stitch the treetop and trunk in place ¼" from the tree edges. Arrange the bear appliqués in the corner openings between the center square and border inner edge as shown. Be sure the bears are facing the correct directions. Pin or spray-baste the bears in

place. Stitch the bears in place ¼" from the bear edges.

9. Cut 2 of the dark green 2" x 42" strips to 2" x 41". Using the marked lines as a guide, position a strip on the center-square top and bottom-border lines, aligning the strips with the inner marked lines. Pin or spray-baste the strips in place. Stitch the strips in place ¼" from the strip edges. Stitch the remaining 2" x 42" strips together end to end to make 1 long strip. From the strip, cut 2 segments, each 2" x 45". Pin or spray-baste the strips to the marked center-square side-border lines. Stitch the strips in place ¼" from the strip edges.

2" x 41"

2" x 45"

10. Cut 2 of the light green 1½" x 42" strips to 1½" x 41½". Set aside. Stitch the remaining light green 1½" x 42" strips together end to end to make 1 continuous strip. From the strip, cut 2 segments, each 1½" x 44½". Center a strip over each side dark green border strip; pin or spray-baste the strips in place. Stitch the strips in place ¼" from the light green strip edges. Center a 1½" x 41½" strip over each top and bottom dark green border strip, going slightly beyond the side border strips; pin or spray-baste the strips in place. Stitch the strips in place ¼" from the light green strip edges.

11. Pin or spray-baste 5 Woven Nine Patch blocks along the outer edge of the upper border line, alternating dark and light blocks as shown. Butt the block edges together. Refer to step 5 to stitch the blocks in place. Position and stitch 5 blocks along the outer edge of the bottom border line in the same manner. Position and stitch 7 blocks along each side border edge, being sure to alternate the block colors. When the quilt is washed and dried, the edges will curl and fray, and the muslin will show through as a narrow sashing.

12. From the remaining dark green pieced strip, cut 2 segments, each 2" x 63", for the top and bottom outer borders, and 2 segments, each 2" x 67", for the side outer borders. Pin or spray-baste the top and bottom segments along the outer edges of the Woven Nine Patch blocks. Stitch the strips in place ¼" from the strip edges. Stitch the side segments in place in the same manner.

13. From the remaining light green pieced strip, cut 2 segments, each 1½" x 66½", for the side outer borders, and 2 segments, each 1½" x 63½", for the top and bottom outer borders. Center a light green side segment over each dark green side segment; pin or spray-baste the segments in place. Stitch the segments in place ¼" from the light green segment edges. Center a light green top and bottom segment over each dark green top and bottom segment, going slightly beyond the side segments; pin or spray-baste the segments in place. Stitch the strips in place ¼" from the light green segment edges.

14. Trim the quilt top, batting, and backing even with the edge of the dark green outer border.

15. Refer to "Washing and Drying the Finished Quilt" on page 21 to wash and dry the quilt. Trim any loose, tangled threads.

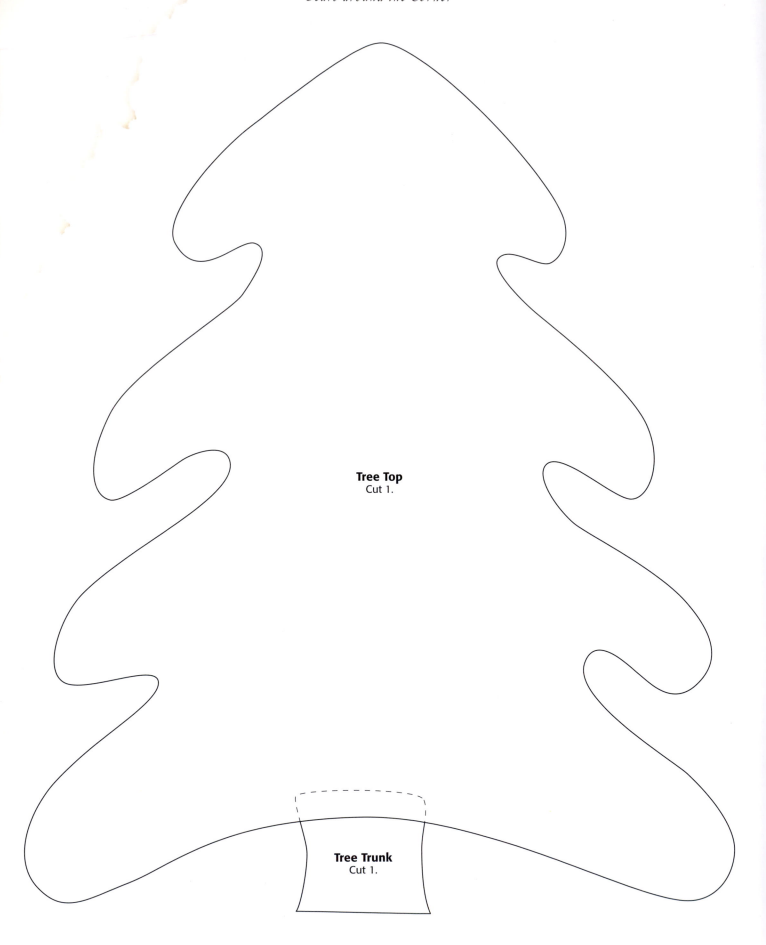

Tree Top
Cut 1.

Tree Trunk
Cut 1.

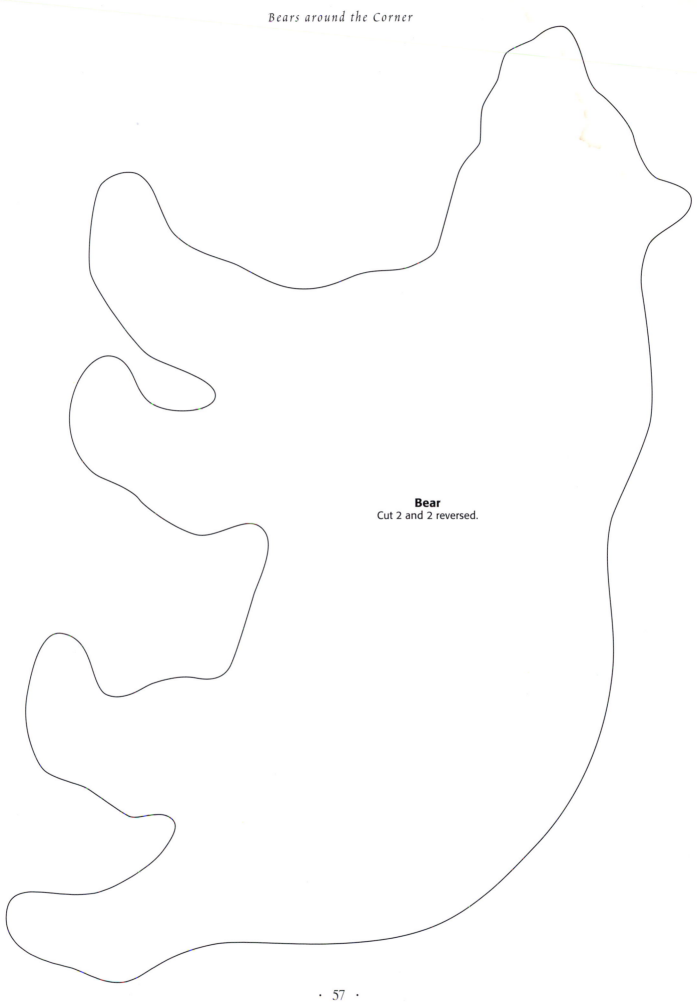

Bear
Cut 2 and 2 reversed.

Baby Blues

<small>FINISHED QUILT SIZE: 41" x 41" · TECHNIQUE: Frayed circles</small>

*Soft blue and yellow prints make this an adorable quilt for a special baby. He or she
will love the cuddly softness and it may even become a comfort quilt that will be enjoyed for many years.
When selecting the fabrics for this quilt, remember that those used for the backs of the circles
will also be seen on the front of the quilt when the flaps are folded back
and stitched down, so all of the fabrics should coordinate.*

Materials

(42" wide fabric)

- 1⅜ yds. *each* of 2 coordinating flannel prints for center-section top circles and backing and front arcs
- 1⅜ yds. *each* of 2 coordinating flannel prints for inner-border top circles and backing and front arcs
- 1½ yds. *each* of 2 coordinating flannel prints for outer-border top circles and backing and front arcs
- Template plastic
- Water-soluble marker or chalk pencil

Cutting

From *each* of the 4 flannel prints for the center section and inner border, cut:

- 5 strips, 8" x 42"

From *each* of the 2 flannel prints for the outer border, cut:

- 6 strips, 8" x 42"

Instructions

Refer to "Frayed Circles" on page 15.

1. Referring to "Making Templates" on page 10, trace the circle and square patterns on pages 61 and 62 onto template plastic. The cutting- and stitching-circle patterns are nested one inside the other, so be sure to trace each one separately. When tracing the cutting-circle pattern, mark the stitching-circle pattern line on the template for alignment purposes. Cut out the templates on the outer lines.

2. Determine which fabrics will be used for the top circles in the center section, the inner border, and the outer border, and which fabrics will be used for the backing and front arcs in the center section, the inner border, and the outer border. With wrong sides together, pin each top-circle fabric strip to a backing-and-front-arc fabric strip. You should have 5 pairs of strips each for the center section and inner border and 6 pairs of strips for the outer border.

3. Using the stitching-circle template and a water-soluble marker or chalk pencil, trace the circles onto the top fabric of each strip, leaving approximately 1" between circles. Trace 25 circles onto the center-section strips, 24 circles onto the inner-border strips, and 28 circles onto the outer-border strips. Place the square template over each of the marked circles so that the corners align with the circle edges. Trace around the template.

4. Stitch completely around each circle on the marked line. Place the cutting-circle template over each circle, aligning the template stitching line with the stitching. Trace around the template. Cut out each circle on the cutting line.

5. Sew the circles together into rows, following the layout diagram carefully. Stitch the rows together, leaving the flaps on the outer edges unstitched.

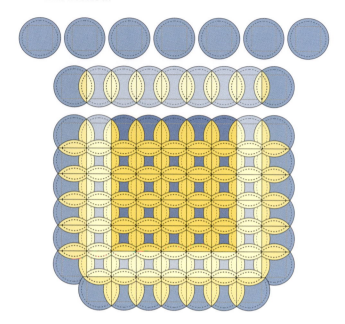

6. Clip all of the seam allowances, as well as the outside edges of the quilt. Make clips about ¼" apart, clipping almost to the stitching line.

7. Refer to "Washing and Drying the Finished Quilt" on page 21 to wash and dry the quilt.

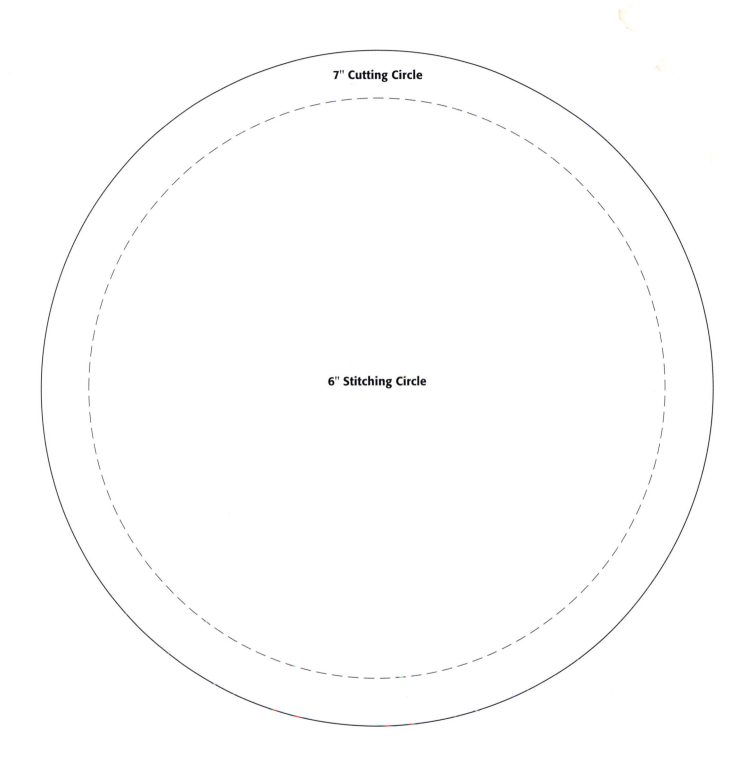

7" Cutting Circle

6" Stitching Circle

4¼" Square

Four-Patch Snuggler and Pillow

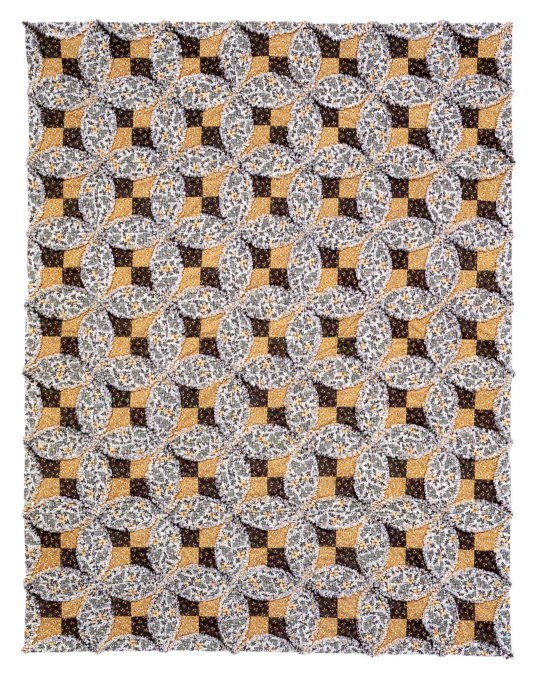

FINISHED QUILT SIZE: 49" x 63" · FINISHED PILLOW SIZE: 20" x 20" · TECHNIQUE: Frayed circles

*Add a little twist to the basic frayed-circles technique by cutting your circles from a four-patch unit.
The illusion created when the flaps are stitched down on the front will have your friends thinking
you've spent loads of time and effort to achieve perfectly curved pieces. In reality, the quilt
goes together so quickly you'll have plenty of time to stitch up a matching pillow—
a perfect duo for snuggling. Thanks to Sharon Pennel for the pillow technique.*

Materials

(42" wide fabric)

FOR THE QUILT

- 4 yds. *each* of 1 light-color flannel print and 1 dark-color flannel print for four-patch units
- 7½ yds. coordinating flannel print for backing and front arcs
- Template plastic
- Water-soluble marker or chalk pencil

FOR THE PILLOW

- 1½ yds. *each* of 1 light-color flannel print and 1 dark-color flannel print for four-patch units
- 2½ yds. coordinating flannel print for backing and front arcs
- Template plastic
- Water-soluble marker or chalk pencil
- Polyester fiberfill (quantity depends on desired firmness)

Cutting

FOR THE QUILT

From *each* of the light- and dark-color flannel prints for four-patch units, cut:

- 21 strips, 6¼" x 42"

From the coordinating flannel print for backing and front arcs, cut:

- 21 strips, 12" x 42"

FOR THE PILLOW

From *each* of the light- and dark-color flannel prints for four-patch units, cut:

- 6 strips, 6¼" x 42"

From the coordinating flannel print for backing and front arcs, cut:

- 6 strips, 12" x 42"

Quilt Instructions

Refer to "Frayed Circles" on page 15.

1. With right sides together, stitch a light 6¼" x 42" strip to a dark 6¼" x 42" strip along the long edges, using a ¼" seam allowance. Press the seam allowance toward the dark strip. Make 21 strip sets. Crosscut the strip sets into 126 segments, each 6¼" wide.

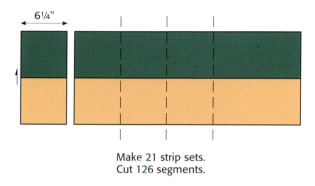

Make 21 strip sets.
Cut 126 segments.

2. Sew 2 segments together as shown to make a four-patch unit. Press the seam allowance in one direction. Make 63 units.

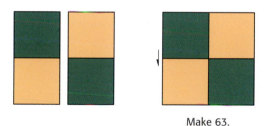

Make 63.

3. Referring to "Making Templates" on page 10, trace the cutting- and stitching-circle patterns on page 69 and the square pattern on page 70 onto template plastic. The cutting- and stitching-circle patterns are shown nested one inside the other and are too large to be shown full size. To make a full-size stitching-circle template, trace the quarter-circle pattern onto template plastic, including the center point.

Rotate the template plastic 90° and trace the next quarter of the circle onto the template plastic. Rotate the template plastic twice more to complete the circle. Trace the cutting-circle pattern onto the template plastic in the same manner. Trace the stitching-circle outer edges onto the cutting-circle template for alignment purposes. Be sure to mark the horizontal and vertical lines on the square template.

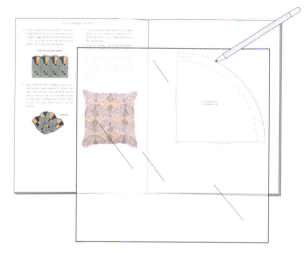

Trace one quarter of the circle.

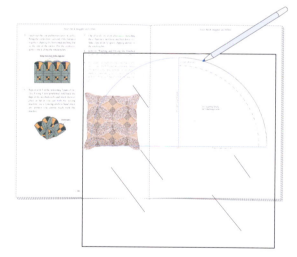

Rotate template plastic 90° and trace next quarter.

4. Place the square template on the right side of each four-patch unit, aligning the horizontal and vertical lines on the template with the four-patch seams. Using a water-soluble marker or chalk pencil, trace around the square.

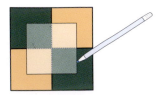

5. Place the stitching-circle template over the marked square on each four-patch unit. The corners of the square should line up with the circle as shown. Trace around the circle with a water-soluble marker or chalk pencil.

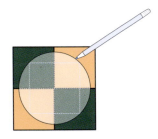

6. Place a 12" x 42" strip of backing fabric wrong side up on a flat surface. With right sides up, lay 3 marked four-patch units side by side on the backing strip, aligning the strip and four-patch edges. Pin the four-patch units in place. Stitch completely around each circle on the marked lines. Place the cutting template over each circle, aligning the template stitching line with the stitching. Trace around the template. Cut out each circle on the cutting line.

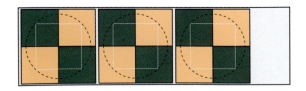

7. Stitch the circles into 9 rows of 7 circles each. Stitch the rows together. Fold the outer circle flaps to the front and stitch them in place to make straight edges.

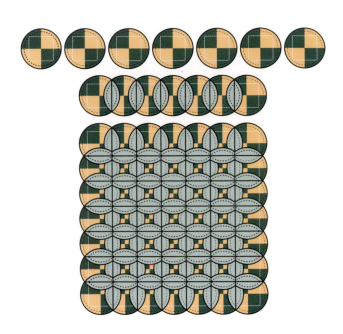

Tip

When you place the two circle units together, if you match up the center seams of the four-patch units, the drawn lines will fall into place.

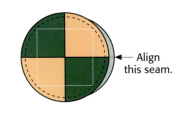

← Align this seam.

8. Clip all of the arc seam allowances. Make clips about ¼" apart, clipping almost to the stitching line.

9. Refer to "Washing and Drying the Finished Quilt" on page 21 to wash and dry the quilt.

Pillow Instructions

Refer to "Frayed Circles" on page 15.

1. Referring to steps 1–6 of the quilt instructions, make 6 strip sets, using the 6¼" x 42" light and dark strips. Crosscut the strip sets to make 32 segments, each 6¼" wide. Make 16 four-patch-unit circles.

2. Stitch the circles into 4 rows of 4 circles each. Sew the rows together, leaving the outer circle flaps unstitched.

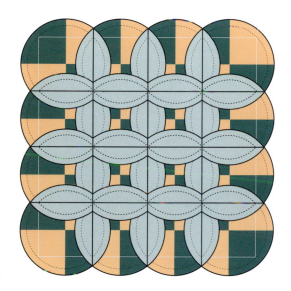

3. Fold the piece in half, backing sides together, matching up the outer circle edges. Stitch the circles at the ends of each row together along the marked square's outer vertical line.

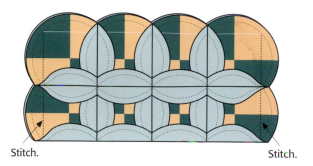

Stitch.   Stitch.

4. Fold the flaps back onto the four-patch circles on both sides of the folded piece. Open out the side seams and stitch the flaps in place as far as you can with the sewing machine; use a running stitch to hand stitch any portion you cannot reach with the machine.

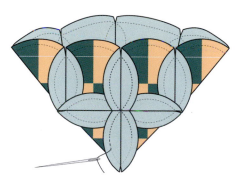

Stitch as far as possible on the machine; then hand stitch flaps to the corner.

5. Open out the top and bottom layer of circles. Bring the circles from each end of the top layer together, aligning the horizontal stitching line at the top of the circles. Pin the circles together; stitch along the stitching line.

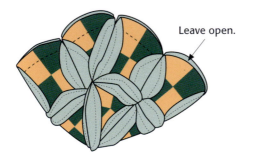

Bring these 2 circles together.

6. Repeat with 2 of the remaining 3 pairs of circles, leaving 1 pair unstitched. Fold back the flaps of the stitched circles and stitch them in place as far as you can with the sewing machine; use a running stitch to hand stitch any portion you cannot reach with the machine.

Leave open.

7. Clip all of the arc seam allowances, including those that have not been stitched down yet. Make clips about ¼" apart, clipping almost to the stitching line.

8. Refer to "Washing and Drying the Finished Quilt" on page 21 to wash and dry the pillow cover.

9. If necessary, re-mark the stitching line on the open circles. Stuff the pillow cover with fiberfill until it is the desired firmness. The seams you have sewn in steps 4–6 should be on the diagonal when you stuff the pillow. Stitch the opening closed along the marked lines, fold back the flaps, and hand stitch the flaps in place.

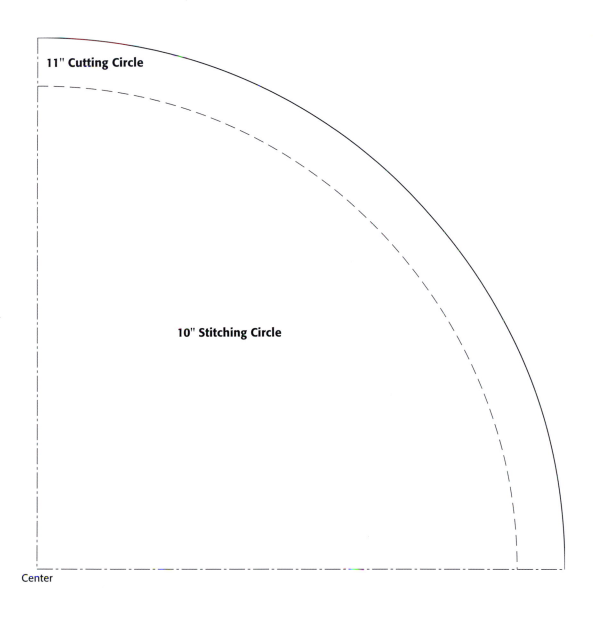

11" Cutting Circle

10" Stitching Circle

Center

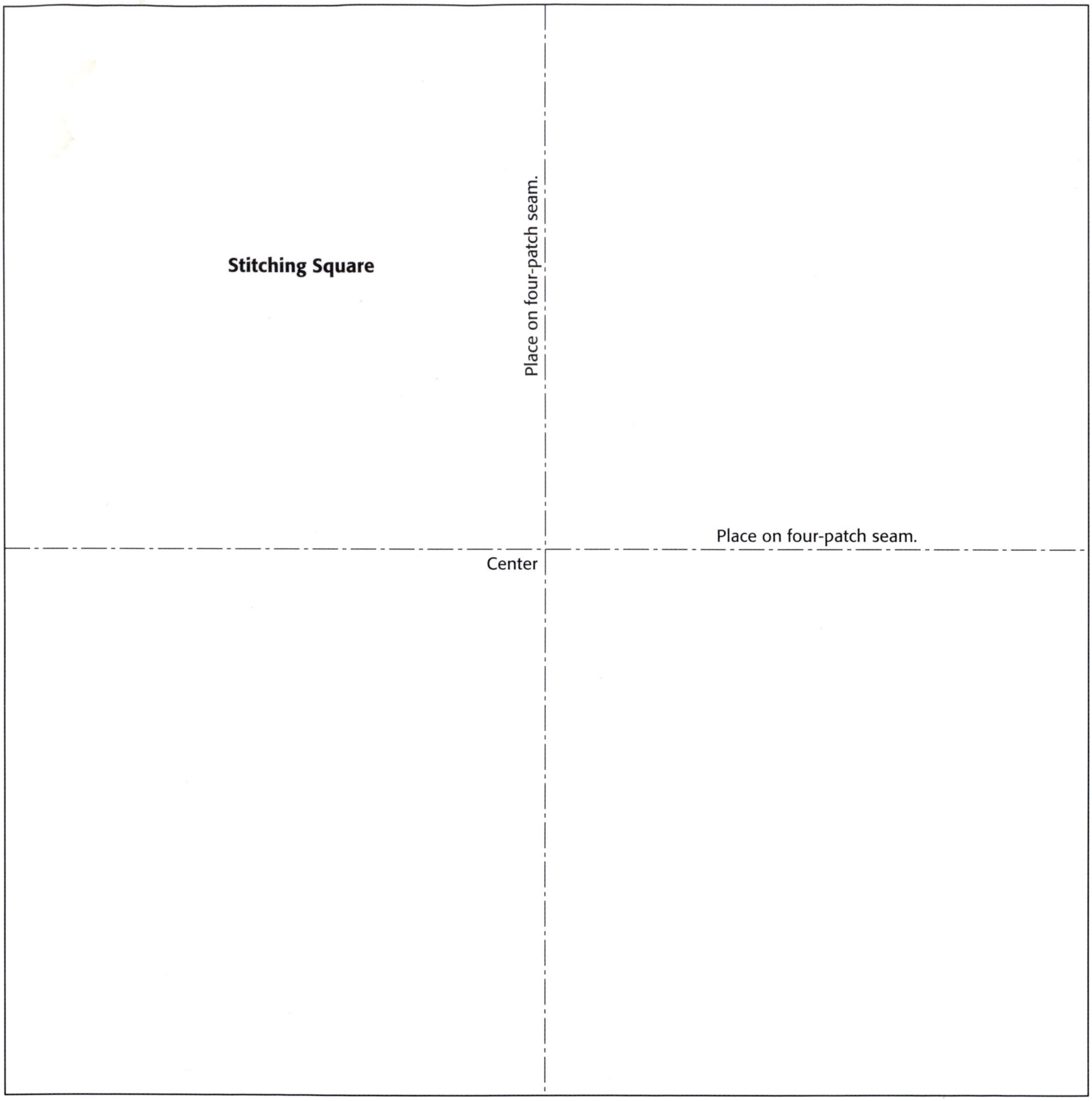

Stitching Square

Place on four-patch seam.

Place on four-patch seam.

Center

Forever Frayed

FINISHED QUILT SIZE: 47" x 66" · TECHNIQUE: Frayed circles

Oval and half-oval shapes are used instead of circles to create this rich-looking quilt.
I used just two different fabrics, but an assortment of light and dark prints would work equally well.

Materials

(42" wide fabric)

- 6½ yds. dark-color flannel print for top
- 6½ yds. light-color flannel print for backing and front arcs
- Template plastic
- Water-soluble marker or chalk pencil

Cutting

From the dark-color flannel print, cut:
- 28 strips, 7½" x 42"

From the light-color flannel print, cut:
- 28 strips, 7½" x 42"

Instructions

Refer to "Frayed Circles" on page 15.

1. Referring to "Making Templates" on page 10, trace the oval, half-oval, and diamond template patterns on pages 75–77 onto template plastic. The oval and half-oval stitching and cutting patterns are nested one inside the other, so be sure to make 2 separate templates for each shape. For alignment purposes, mark the oval stitching-pattern line on the oval cutting template; mark the half-oval stitching-pattern line on the half-oval cutting template. Cut out the templates on the outer lines.

2. With wrong sides together, pin each dark-print strip to a light-print strip. Using the oval stitching template and a water-soluble marker or chalk pencil, trace 97 ovals onto the dark-print side of the strip pairs, leaving at least 1" between the shapes. You should be able to trace 4 ovals onto a strip.

3. Place the diamond template over each of the marked ovals so that the diamond corners align with the oval edges. Trace around the diamond. Stitch completely around the oval on the drawn line. Place the oval cutting template over each stitched oval, aligning the template stitching line with the stitching. Trace around the template. Cut out each oval on the cutting line.

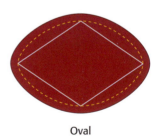

Oval

4. Using the half-oval stitching template and a water-soluble marker or chalk pencil, trace 16 half ovals onto the dark-print side of the remaining strip pairs. Position the diamond template over each half oval so that 1 end point and 2 side points align with the narrow end of the half oval as shown. Trace half of the diamond onto the half oval. Stitch completely around each half oval on the marked line. Place the half-oval cutting template over each stitched half oval, aligning the template stitching line with the stitching. Trace around the template. Cut out each half oval on the cutting line.

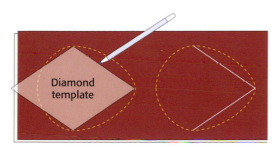

Trace half of diamond onto half ovals.

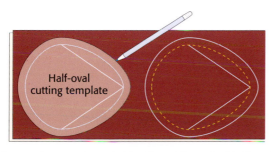

Align cutting-template stitching line with stitched half oval.

Half Oval

5. Stitch the ovals and half ovals into 15 diagonal rows, referring to the diagram on page 74 for the placement of the half ovals. Pin the pieces together, backing fabric to backing fabric, so the upper right marked line of the diamond on the left piece is aligned with the lower left marked line of the diamond on the right piece. Stitch along the marked line. Finger-press the flaps open and stitch them in place.

Stitch the rows together, leaving the outer flaps unstitched.

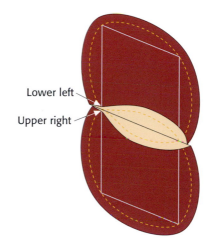

6. Clip all of the seam allowances, as well as the outside edges of the quilt. Make clips about ¼" apart, clipping almost to the stitching line.

7. Refer to "Washing and Drying the Finished Quilt" on page 21 to wash and dry the quilt.

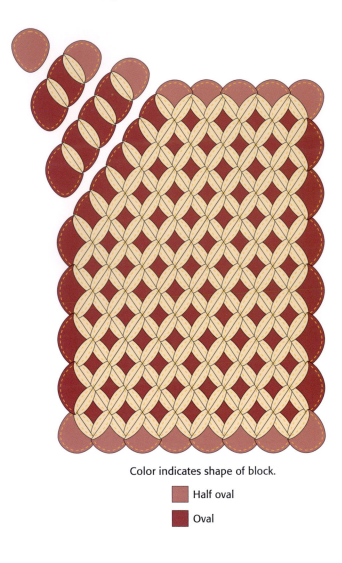

Color indicates shape of block.

Half oval

Oval

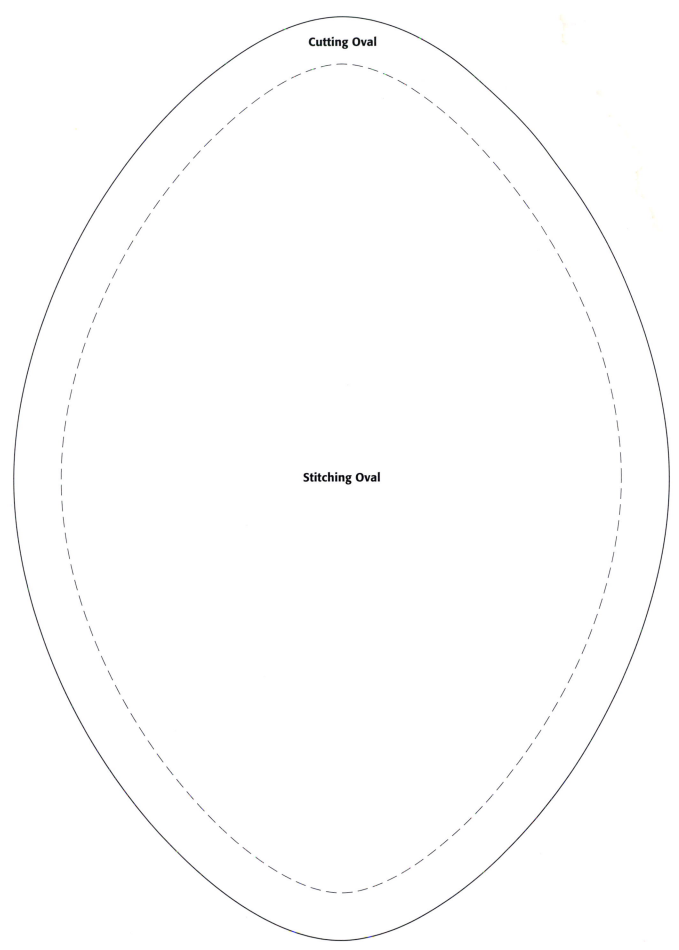

Cutting Oval

Stitching Oval

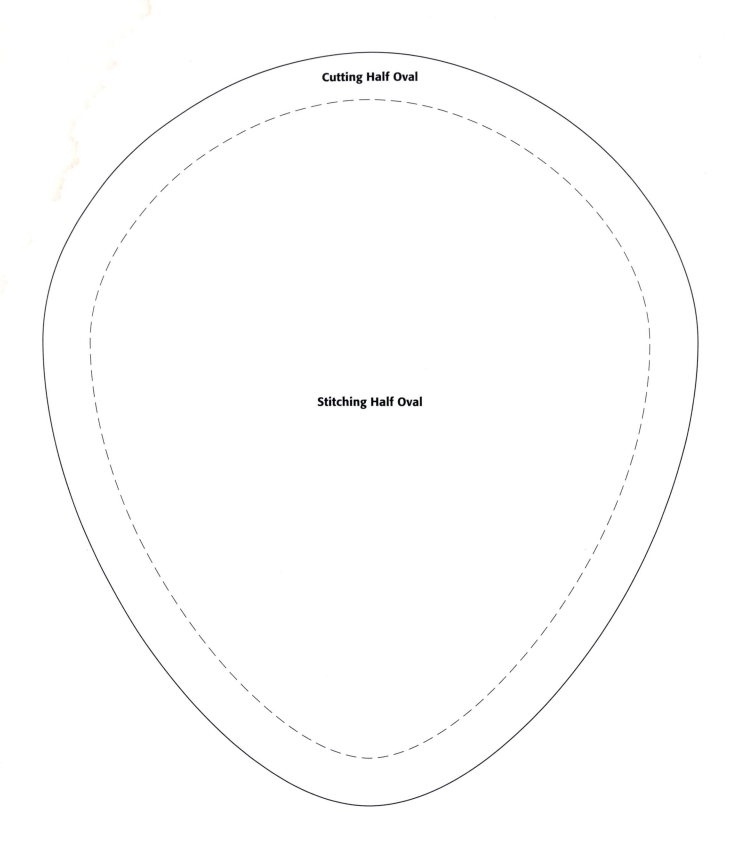

Cutting Half Oval

Stitching Half Oval

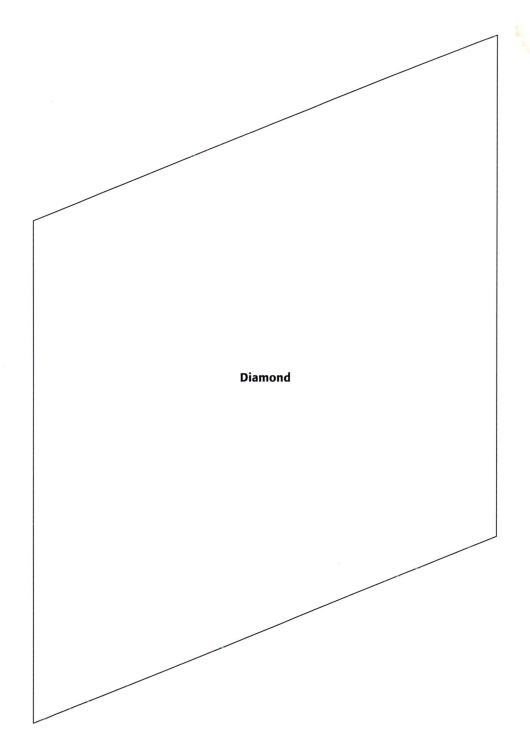

Diamond

About the Author

Evelyn Sloppy lives with her husband, Dean, on eighty wooded acres in western Washington, where she savors the peaceful country life and visits from their four children and four grandchildren. She has been quilting since 1991 and has enjoyed designing her own quilts and teaching at several area quilt shops since 1998. Her quilting interests are broad, but she especially enjoys making scrappy, traditional quilts. *Frayed Edge Fun* follows on the heels of *Log Cabin Fever*, also published by Martingale & Company.

new and bestselling titles from

Martingale™
& C O M P A N Y

America's Best-Loved Craft & Hobby Books™

That Patchwork Place®

America's Best-Loved Quilt Books®

NEW RELEASES
Bear's Paw Plus
All through the Woods
American Quilt Classics
Amish Wall Quilts
Animal Kingdom CD-ROM
Batik Beauties
The Casual Quilter
Fantasy Floral Quilts
Fast Fusible Quilts
Friendship Blocks
From the Heart
Log Cabin Fever
Machine-Stitched Cathedral Stars
Magical Hexagons
Quilts From Larkspur Farm
Potting Shed Patchwork
Repliqué Quilts
Successful Scrap Quilts
   from Simple Rectangles

APPLIQUÉ
Artful Album Quilts
Artful Appliqué
Colonial Appliqué
Red and Green: An Appliqué Tradition
Rose Sampler Supreme

BABY QUILTS
Easy Paper-Pieced Baby Quilts
Even More Quilts for Baby: Easy as ABC
More Quilts for Baby: Easy as ABC
Play Quilts
The Quilted Nursery
Quilts for Baby: Easy as ABC

HOLIDAY QUILTS
Christmas at That Patchwork Place
Holiday Collage Quilts
Paper Piece a Merry Christmas
A Snowman's Family Album Quilt
Welcome to the North Pole

LEARNING TO QUILT
Basic Quiltmaking Techniques for:
   Borders and Bindings
   Divided Circles
   Hand Appliqué
   Machine Appliqué
   Strip Piecing
The Joy of Quilting
The Simple Joys of Quilting
Your First Quilt Book (or it should be!)

PAPER PIECING
50 Fabulous Paper-Pieced Stars
For the Birds
Paper Piece a Flower Garden
Paper-Pieced Bed Quilts
Paper-Pieced Curves
A Quilter's Ark
Show Me How to Paper Piece

ROTARY CUTTING
101 Fabulous Rotary-Cut Quilts
365 Quilt Blocks a Year Perpetual Calendar
Around the Block Again
Biblical Blocks
Creating Quilts with Simple Shapes
Flannel Quilts
More Fat Quarter Quilts
More Quick Watercolor Quilts
Razzle Dazzle Quilts

SCRAP QUILTS
Nickel Quilts
Scrap Frenzy
Scrappy Duos
Spectacular Scraps

CRAFTS
The Art of Stenciling
Baby Dolls and Their Clothes
Creating with Paint
The Decorated Kitchen
The Decorated Porch
A Handcrafted Christmas
Painted Chairs
Sassy Cats

KNITTING & CROCHET
Too Cute!
Clever Knits
Crochet for Babies and Toddlers
Crocheted Sweaters
Fair Isle Sweaters Simplified
Irresistible Knits
Knit It Your Way
Knitted Shawls, Stoles, and Scarves
Knitted Sweaters for Every Season
Knitting with Novelty Yarns
Paintbox Knits
Simply Beautiful Sweaters
Simply Beautiful Sweaters for Men
The Ultimate Knitter's Guide

Our books are available at bookstores and your favorite craft, fabric and yarn retailers. If you don't see the title you're looking for, visit us at www.martingale-pub.com or contact us at:

1-800-426-3126

International: 1-425-483-3313

Fax: 1-425-486-7596

E-mail: info@martingale-pub.com

For more information and a full list of our titles, visit our Web site or call for a free catalog.